To Alan, Christmas 1963
Though I miss "those days" more
than you – M.

THOSE DAYS

THOSE DAYS

by Hamilton Fish Armstrong

hours too sweet for spending
like curled leaves unfolding,
breath too quick for breathing,
heart too big for holding,
in days that had no ending . . .

Those days.

—MARION EDEY

HARPER & ROW, PUBLISHERS
NEW YORK, EVANSTON, AND LONDON

"Thomas Jefferson" by Stephen Vincent Benét is from *A Book of Americans* by Rosemary and Stephen Vincent Benét, published by Holt, Rinehart & Winston, Inc.

FIRST EDITION

G-N

LIBRARY OF CONGRESS CATALOG CARD NUMBER: 63-16502

FOR

HELEN, JANE, SARAH

AND DAVID

Into the double glass I look
And see in lessening line
Myself repeated endlessly—
Or almost,
For at the farthest rim beyond which no eye travels
Clings a last tiny shape.
Is that me too?
That shadowy reproduction,
Distant, remote,
As in my self in boyhood
When all those other selves had not been interposed
Between my incandescent innocence
And what I am now seven decades gone?
Each span a larger picture shows;
And each one clearer in the glass
Less to my liking is.
Yet from the curving mirror's deep recess
I catch a small refrain,
Distant antiphonal salute,
Muffled but cheerful,
Passing along through half-remembered time
The eagerness for truth and beauty once I knew.

≈ I ≈

A boy's will is the wind's will,
And the thoughts of youth are long, long thoughts
—LONGFELLOW

≈ THE TIME WHEN WE ARE VERY YOUNG IS THE ONLY
thing shorter than the sum of its parts. Suddenly it is
gone; yet each bit of colored glass that settles down at
last to make the pattern of the whole has held its place
in the kaleidoscope for a moment that seemed endless.
The dark hour in bed while the family are at dinner in
a far part of the house; the droning sermon (why can't
he just say "Be good! Be good!" and finish?); Lent with
mite boxes and no candy; the moon's slow course across
the winter sky, measured with squinty eye as it moves
from one crack between the cedar trees to another; that
last round of Buffalo Bill's unsuspecting stagecoach in
Madison Square Garden with the Indians lurking right
there in the entrance—each by itself has seemed to go
on forever.

How slowly the light creeps in to reveal in angular
outline the Christmas stocking that last night hung
limply under the mantelpiece and now sprawls bloatedly

against the fender with a chair alongside to prop it up. Will St. Valentine's Day never bring the postman's whistle and his packet of envelopes with scrawled addresses? Will they never arrive for the birthday party, to pin on the donkey's tail and hunt for Easter eggs? Will that wobbly front tooth never let go, no matter how hard you suck at it in hopes of escaping the string and doorknob?

In June the summer shimmers ahead endlessly—streams to be dammed, crayfish to be caught, blackberries to be picked, books to be read, fudge to be made on rainy days (why don't the drops in the tumbler get chewy?), Indians lying in ambush for the white men in the high corn, Slap Jack with Mary McGuire in the kitchen if she has time before supper. On the Fourth, Papa's ban on noise before seven seems incredibly hardhearted: from five o'clock on, the kitchen clock, brought along for frequent consultation, moves so slowly as to raise grave doubts whether it isn't broken.

Then almost at once, for no special cause and on no special date, what in each part has been endless is ended. Minutes and hours no longer are things in themselves, palpable like the puckering of chokecherries or the sweet smell of lumber in the sawmill, but mere installments of passing time, useful in calculating profit and waste. In the days of which I am writing, though, such measurements lay aeons ahead.

❧ II ❧

Oh what fun to have a plum bun!
How I wis it never was done!

—BETSINDA, in
"The Rose and the Ring"

❧ MY FIRST CLEAR PICTURE IS OF MARCHING MEN. I am peering down into Fifth Avenue through a balcony railing of the old Grosvenor, on the corner of Tenth Street. It is the fall of 1896, I am three years old, and this is the great "sound-money" parade in which all right-thinking New York is protesting against the free-silver heresies of William Jennings Bryan. Businessmen, merchants, stockbrokers, clerks and college students have been gathering downtown since noon and are now moving north from Washington Square, line after line, hour after hour, uninteresting-looking citizens in ordinary clothes with only a very occasional band for diversion. Seen from above, the derby hats are like bulbous black vegetables, row after row of them monotonously repeated.

It is a decided comedown from what I had expected of a parade. My mother's friend, Mrs. Lawton, from whose apartment we are watching, assuages my disappointment with cambric tea and cake, and a present which at a later date I realized was appropriate to the occasion—a locket containing grains of gold brought back by her father, Major Robert Anderson of Fort Sumter fame, from an early expedition to Alaska, the first indication of the wealth which the next summer would be luring thousands in the great Klondike rush.

Suddenly as it gets dark and time for me to be taken home the scene is transformed. The marchers light torches, thousands of them, and with fresh energy begin shouting out their fury against free-silver Bryan and their love for sound-money McKinley. The air thickens with smoke and the smell of pitch. The slogans reach our balcony in a confused roar. The excitement is incomprehensible but contagious, and for some time my dreams will be full of derby-hatted hobgoblins.

The next day I was given a "Gold Bug" pin to wear on my Russian blouse. As the political campaign progressed my interest in the discussions became intense and as usual I was eager to participate. My opinion as to the probable winner was as good as most political prophecies:

"I *hope* it will be Fitzsimmons, but I'm *afraid* it will be Corbett."

About this time I began shouldering what I considered an important responsibility. There was a firehouse only a block away from where we lived in Tenth Street. Whenever I heard an engine coming I would rush to the window and watch it safely by, whistle screaming in uneven jerks, the three horses galloping abreast, the men on the rear step squirming into their slickers, clouds of smoke fuming out of the polished nickel stack.

After dark the blazing excelsior and kindling in the monster's belly turned the smoke an angry red. I was certain it went about setting fires, and if it were to stop at our house my duty would be to give the alarm.

Our house was really two little houses made into one by my father in the 1880's, leaving many stairs, landings and passageways, excellent for games though hard on the maids, both because they had to toil up and down them and sweep in so many corners and because you could pop out at them unawares and, as they complained resignedly, be after scarin' the livin' daylights out of them. The house had several sets of everything. There were three roofs to be kept tight and cleared of winter snows and two cellars with two coal furnaces to be tended. The kitchen was separated from the dining room by a flight of stairs, a passageway, another flight of stairs and a pantry. Other arrangements which would be equally impossible today were not thought of then as even inconvenient. Twelve fireplaces, most of them log-burning but several with Franklin stoves or grates for soft coal, supplemented the hot air which flowed from registers in the floor and supplied a pleasant warmth up one's canton-flannel nightshirt and, my sisters said, was equally agreeable under a billowing skirt. The impractical features of the house did not worry Papa in the least. He was a man of taste and originality, and how things looked mattered to him far more than whether they were utilitarian.

The two houses which he bought and joined were not alongside but one in front of the other. The rear house, which must have been built about 1830, stood in the middle of the block with nothing but garden between it and the street until another little house was built in front, perhaps twenty years later. In order that it should not be isolated, a sort of tunnel was left through the basement of the front house. The older house kept its original doorway, hung with wisteria, opening on its own scrap of garden full of New York's always optimistic ailanthus trees. When my father first knew it, this was the entrance to the Tile Club, an artists' meeting place.

The club did not take its name from the white tiles framing the two fireplaces, designed by Stanford White, but from the experiments of several artists who had been painting on tiles and potsherds with the vitreous paints invented by Lacroix.* It became a fad to meet here, shut off from the city's noises, and, as was rudely said, "punish" unoffending crockery (as Picasso did a couple of generations later). Other artists joined—Homer, Chase, Saint-Gaudens, Weir and others of that day—not to punish crockery but to gather in the evening to talk, smoke, eat oysters with hock or mallards with Burgundy, dispute each other's ideas and criticize each other's paintings. My father went there sometimes with friends; and when the club dissolved he acquired both houses, did them over and joined them across the yard by constructing what we called the parlor (a word not yet the property of beauticians and morticians). It was a formidable undertaking for an artist with a large family and very limited means, but he was never abashed by difficulties or afraid of hard work and he must have had great fun out of what amounted to building a new house. The moldings, mantels and white paneling were

* *A Book of the Tile Club.* Boston: Houghton, Mifflin, 1887.

after his own design, and he and White and other friends modeled the bas-relief detail on the spot from plaster of Paris.

What had attracted him particularly was the fine studio over the Tile Club, occupied in succession by two artist friends, first Edwin Abbey, then Hopkinson Smith, an engineer by profession but also an artist and writer. Hop Smith used the two houses as the scene of his best-known novel, *Colonel Carter of Cartersville,* and his drawings of the two front doors, 58 on the street and 58½ on the yard, continue to hang in the hall—for I live there still. I once thought that an easy way to become president of something would be to form a society of New Yorkers still inhabiting the houses where they were born, but I could discover no members.

My family had settled down here several years before I came along, but visitors still would exclaim how "interesting" it was, how "different" to eyes accustomed to brownstone fronts and Victorian black walnut, varnished oak, Oriental nooks, beaded curtains, plush, horsehair and green rep. Among the daring features were the white trim on the red-brick front, much copied afterwards in the neighborhood, the wide hall window of small leaded panes, and the mahogany door on which was fixed a griffin knocker with spread wings and extended talons, very decorative but apt to claw the hair or hats of visitors. When these innovations were finished everybody stopped to stare. It took less to astound people then; the Flatiron Building was still twenty-five years in the future, the Guggenheim "ziggurat" more than seventy-five.

The griffin had been bought in Venice in 1869, during the time my father was living in Rome as consul to the Papal States; it was one of a pair, the other being still in the Doge's Palace. In those years he acquired a quantity of *roba di Roma* which a generation later he could not possibly have been able to afford; for that was still the time when Americans on the Grand Tour went home with reproductions of the "Dying Gaul" and marbles by Rogers or Story to place under their paintings by Durand and Huntington. One of Rogers' most successful statues was of Lydia, the blind girl of Pompeii, depicted as listening intently, groping her way with a staff. "I once went to his studio," my father wrote, "and saw seven Lydias, all in a row, all listening, all groping, and seven Italian marble-cutters at work cutting them. It was a gruesome sight."

I liked everything about the house except perhaps the griffin, even though he was fixed too high up to be able to grab me. I liked there being so many levels and plenty of stairs to dash up and down; the enormous kitchen with the range set in a recess where a Dutch oven had once been; the deep, narrow bathtub, like a sarcophagus, raised on four claws, with sponge pleasantly slimy from soap and wooden-cased thermometer floating among a flock of carved animals from Switzerland, surviving remarkably well an aqueous life they had not been made for and worn to bone-whiteness; the toilets that rushed noisily at the pull of the chain and recuperated with protracted friendly gurglings; the bedroom gas jets on two-jointed arms, with almost human maneuverability; the gramophone with lily horn and cylindrical wax rolls, kept wrapped in cotton wool in small cartons, which played (over and over as long as the family could stand it) "My Old Kentucky Home" and mournful "Old Black Joe." I liked the white folding doors of my nursery which provided an excellent expanse on which to exhibit, entrance fee one pin, the slides of my one-candlepower (literally) magic lantern. The favorite was a three-panel slide, dim with smoke but otherwise almost as good as a moving picture, showing in successive jerks a train approaching a tunnel, the caboose disappearing into it and the engine emerging at the other end. I liked the sunny roof over the parlor where on spring days I could lug out a small chair and table and draw pictures (of no artistic promise whatsoever) or set in order my many animals which ranged from a large papier-mâché speckled spider to a green tin parrot.

Why a certain toy becomes a favorite cannot be explained, certainly by a grownup. Mine was the parrot, even though it was (or because it was) only an empty shell. Once it had run on wheels, but by the time it became indispensable to me waking or sleeping, it had lost them and could be pulled along the sidewalk with an agreeable scraping sound. Sometimes Mamma would take me shopping in the morning. Her skirts, which were very full and swept the ground, were lined at the bottom with black braid, changed constantly for cleanliness, and held up on one side by a loop for a finger of her left hand. To this loop I was supposed to cling, while my parrot clanked along on a string behind. After one expedition I returned parrotless and that night could not sleep. My mother supposed it had dropped off unnoticed in the street (I was sure some envious person had stolen it), and I felt like a parent who had failed to watch properly over a child and as punishment would never see it again. Several days later I almost burst with joy when, in passing Dean's, on Broadway near Nineteenth Street, I spied it in the very front and center of the window, displacing, so that it would surely catch my eye, the customary three-tiered white wedding cake.

Today no city children are born at home, and if the parents are well-to-do the doctor and hospital may charge around a thousand dollars. For seeing to my birth in Tenth Street our Dr. Stimson—an uncle of Secretary Stimson—probably sent a bill of fifteen or twenty dollars. I must have come as a surprise (my mother was forty-eight, my father fifty-six) and certainly as an inconvenience, since my nurse and I made nine, plus servants, in a house that would hold five or six comfortably. My nearest brother, Noel, was eleven already, and the family were looking forward to the time when they could get him off to boarding school and take over his third-floor hall bedroom. My arrival set things back. The surprise to my sister Marion, then thirteen, was literal and complete. Coming downstairs to early breakfast before school she found Papa already dressed standing on the landing outside Mamma's door. He informed her that she had acquired a baby brother. Was it due to Victorian reticences or the voluminous dress of the period? Or was it Marion's ability to ignore anything that did not concern her directly? Whatever the reason, the news struck her like a bolt from the blue, and she went off to school more mystified than ever about the processes of the human race.

To make room for a nursery, my older sisters Margaret

and Helen doubled up, until at last Noel did go off to school and I inherited the hall bedroom, a lovely place where both the bureau and the bookcase were within reach from bed. In the fashion of the day, but partly, perhaps, because my mother may have hoped for a girl as being less trouble, I was at first kept in dresses. Very light long hair, lighter even than tow-colored, must have added to an impression which luckily I was too young to let trouble me. At about three, the skirts gave way to Russian blouses, embroidered in cross-stitch down the side where the buttons are; after these, at five or six, came blue-serge sailor suits for everyday in the city, with short trousers, horrible black ribbed stockings and high button shoes. I was out of dresses and therefore at least three when Elsie Littell, an old family friend, reports her first sight of me standing under a console table in the parlor singing "Sweet Wosy O'Gwady."

I still had not mastered my *r*'s when I went to Miss Lane's school, really a kindergarten, in a high-stoop red-brick house in Twelfth Street. Besides the *r*'s that came out as *w*'s, the *g*'s came out as *b*'s. For some time the family had the impression that my favorite teacher was Miss Wubbles. Papa had taken me there in advance to see Miss Lane but when the first day of school came I insisted on going around there alone, as befitted my dignity of five. I liked the way Miss Ruggles read the Longfellow poem about Agassiz's boyhood in Switzerland, but one by Tennyson caused shivers:

> The splendour falls on castle walls
> And snowy summits old in story:
> The long light shakes across the lakes,
> And the wild cataract leaps in glory.

It must be a splendid animal, I thought, to have such a splendid name. But was it a friendly animal, like the one in the hymn, "Can a woman's tender care, Cease toward the child she bare"? I liked the smooth wooden bear which I took into my bath. But a cataract? I wondered about it as I lay that night between the sheets. The family were far away, down a flight of stairs, beyond the empty library and the empty parlor, where no call would travel. The last chunk of soft coal in the Franklin stove split open with a crack, a friendly blue flame sprang up and the fender made fence patterns on the ceiling. Then came a tinkle of china and I knew the family were back in the parlor having coffee. Soon Mamma came "to see if I were asleep," knowing, of course, that I was not. She sat down quietly and began:

> Close little weary eyes,
> Day's the time for doing,
> The boats lie on the sands,
> The mill-wheels are not turning.

Before the end of the familiar verses I was asleep, and if I dreamed of Miss Ruggles she did not have the wild cataract with her.

Marion, the youngest of my three older sisters, was assigned the ungrateful task of helping along my education. She read with me and spelt with me, she accompanied me on the piano when I learnt hymns in Lent (one a week), and she even tried briefly to teach me to play it—a little Este upright, a shiny mahogany incongruity, crowded into a corner of the parlor during the couple of years when Marion was supposed (though never by herself) to be musical. As we were both impatient none of this worked.

On top of the piano were a metronome to guide her practice and a stuffed pheasant shot by Papa on Gardiners Island; its tail wagged in time, not with the metronome but with Marion's desperate efforts to keep up with it. I could carry a tune and had enough imitative ability to get by heart quite quickly the hymns I heard so often in church. My favorite for aesthetic reasons was "Now the Day Is Over," with its long-drawn wail at the end of the second line. Next, because it was so easy, though grim as befitted Lent, was "Christian dost thou see them, On the holy ground?"—which throughout the first two lines sticks doggedly on the same one note. But to learn even the first thing about the piano took more patience, to say nothing of talent, than I possessed, and the whole vain idea was soon abandoned.

Spelling was hard enough, and my progress was slow, as a picture I executed on wrapping paper evinced when I came across it years later, sere and crackling, lining a top closet shelf. From a large round head sprouting rays like a sun there dangled an immensely long body with emaciated arms and legs, as El Greco or Modigliani might have drawn it in babyhood if totally without talent. This figure towered above a jagged row of mountains, and underneath was written in capitals, "DOG" (a mere error in arranging the letters), and somewhat smaller, "Hav Murcy on Us." Lenten litanies had sunk in deeper than Marion's spelling.

❦ III ❦

Why do I love New York, my dear?
I know not. Were my father here—
And his—and his—the three and I
Might, perhaps, make you some reply.
                                    —H. C. BUNNER

❦ MY MOTHER WAS QUITE TYPICALLY "NEW YORK"
—the New York of wide brownstone houses with high
stoops and high ceilings, carriages to supplement but
not replace the pleasures of walking, constant visits back
and forth among relatives, large Sunday dinners followed by long amusementless Sunday afternoons. It
was a small but not uncultivated society. Her father,
John Neilson, painted, wrote stories and poetry, made
translations from the French for *The Talisman*, was a
friend of the writers and artists of the day, especially
Bryant and the painters Inman and Huntington. He belonged to the Sketch Club (parent of the present Century) whose members met at each other's houses to write
stories or poems and make sketches on subjects suggested on the spur of the moment.

His diary records an even but nevertheless varied life:

shooting snipe with Bryant on the Weehawken Flats or picnicking with him in the woods at Flatbush, visiting the exhibitions of the National Academy or the National Academy of Design, buying land and building houses, attending meetings of the Society Library stockholders or of the vestry of the Church of the Ascension, having his silhouette cut by M. Edouart, attending the "large and respectable funeral" of this or that relative, helping to organize a fund for the suffering Irish, going to see a Raeburn and then a Carlo Dolci (and liking the former better), translating Chateaubriand, attending a benefit for John Howard Payne (back in America and swamped with debts), taking the children "to see the giraffes" or "The Panorama of Jerusalem" or to visit the *Great Western*. One day he might be dining at the house of his uncle, P. G. Stuyvesant, "on the occasion of the 200th Anniversary of Governor Stuyvesant's entering on his administration"; another he would meet his friend Samuel Morse at Delmonico's and record the fear that he was doomed to many disappointments. "I do not think," he wrote, "that, in this country, at least, there is sufficient demand for telegraphic communication to warrant the cost of his apparatus."

The city my mother grew up in, then, was small and in some respects provincial, the pleasures were simple, but the company could be good. Her circle of friends and relatives was probably as large as that of most New Yorkers today and was fully as animated even if not as perpetually interrupted by goings to or comings from somewhere at a distance. Everyone had cousins in quantity; my mother had seventy-two first cousins, and as her family had been in New York for five or six generations most of them considered it the only place to live, and did so. She had known most of her friends all her life and her parents had known theirs also. Entertaining was done at home; restaurants were mainly for unfortunate out-of-towners. In hot weather one went to visit for a few days on the Hudson, perhaps with cousins at Fishkill, or to stay with other cousins at Ursino, near Elizabethtown, or with the Morrisses, also cousins, at Pelham or Morrisania (my father met my mother there, just as his father had met his mother there). Or perhaps one went up the River by boat and thence by coach and four to Geneseo or some other watering place, or beyond to the Niagara. Further Long Island was a heathen waste of sand and scrub oak.

Daguerreotypes and the little photographs named in the fifties and sixties *"cartes de visite"* show that my mother's reputation for beauty as a girl was deserved. Her hair was light, between brown and gold, her eyes were blue-green, set off by eyebrows that were dark and sharply defined. She had a tiny waist, sixteen inches, as evidenced by a costume made for a fancy-dress ball in Rome in 1870, preserved in the "fancy dress chest" in Tenth Street. I can't say that she had quite the same figure forty or so years later, when I was growing up, but she still had a high color and would become even rosier when she was either amused or annoyed.

My father, on the other hand, was only partly New York; the rest was Southern and Scottish. His mother's father was a Charlestonian, and that meant, as old Captain "Tawm" Pinckney once assured me, that if you were related to "anybody" you were related to "everybody." His paternal grandfather, a colonel in the British

Army, had fought up and down the Hudson in the Revolution, lost an eye at Stony Point and visited Newburgh under a flag of truce to deliver a message to Washington. Wars being a professional affair in those days, with no personal feelings involved, he saw nothing strange in selling his commission after surrendering with Cornwallis at Yorktown, cozily marrying the daughter of one of his very recent antagonists and making his home thenceforth among his erring ex-countrymen. He had prided himself on his swordsmanship and marksmanship, and in retirement in New York he maintained his skill in the latter. His duelling pistols were reputed to be as nearly perfect as firearms could be. The last time he lent them was to a friend who was to serve as a second in an affair of honor, the principals not identified; it was the last time because the duel in which one of them was used proved to be that between Aaron Burr and Alexander Hamilton. What was significant to Colonel Armstrong, however, was not that his pistol had killed Alexander Hamilton but that a small x had been carved on the butt to identify it; this, he asserted, "destroyed the balance." (My nephew Noel now has this brace of pistols.)

When his son Edward thought of building a country house, Colonel Armstrong recommended the region above Newburgh—"as pleasant a land," Henry Hudson had written, "as one need tread upon." In fact, the spot chosen was one to which Hudson himself had given a name (therefore among the oldest on our continent) when the *Half Moon,* sailing up the river, dropped anchor one evening in a cove formed by a high level rock, a sickle of sand and a neck of land covered with

17

cedars and wild grapes. Indians were cavorting around bonfires on the rock and Hudson named it "Duyvil's Danskammer"—"Devil's Ballroom."

On a bluff about half a mile south of Danskammer Point my grandfather built a large stone house in the classic style, a Grecian temple, with a portico of six massive columns, looking south across Newburgh Bay to the Highlands, banked in the rear by wooded hills and with long lawns sloping down to the River, then a chief artery of commerce dotted with sails of all sizes. The columns were of granite, brought down by barge from Breakneck, with pearly trim from Quincy. The drums were so large that they could not be gotten up the hill until someone thought of making them into rollers, with axles inserted in the ends, and drawing them slowly by two teams of oxen. Inside, the house was mainly black walnut, then "newer than mahogany."

My grandfather was a man of some accomplishments: he drew and wrote poetry (everyone in that time seemed to do this), played the violin, was a good shot, raised race horses, made a study of medicine and could cut a double pigeon wing. He died within a few years, when my father, the youngest of the family, was only four. My grandmother continued to live at Danskammer, supervised the farm, did delicate and accurate water-colors of fruits and flowers (for which her neighbor, Mr. Downing, the landscape architect, wrote in the names), and brought up her four sons, I won't say to her full satisfaction, for two of them were restless and adventurous enough to be worrisome.

Though my father was small in stature he was strong, wiry and, I suspect, pretty belligerent. But he was not cocky, as small men sometimes are, and though he had a high temper I don't remember in my time his ever really losing it. His brothers taught him to spar from earliest boyhood; he also was a good rider and a good shot. As the boys ranged the woods around Danskammer, an old hunting ground of the Mohawks, they made up a whistle and used it to keep in touch:

The first phrase reported from one spot, the second answered from another. Though the forest has now been farmland for a century the call survives. Not so the tomahawk given to Colonel Armstrong by Joseph Brant, the Mohawk chief and British ally; the boys kept it by the cold spring to crack butternuts and it fell in.

In the winters my grandmother's custom was to travel south in her coach to spend a month or so in Charleston with the relatives whom she entertained in profusion at Danskammer the rest of the year. My father wrote: "I remember very well the two large travelling carriages that used to stand in our stable, arranged for four horses, with a high seat for the coachman, with a big hammer cloth below, and platforms behind for footmen and luggage, and flights of folding steps that let down from inside." The journey to Carolina took more weeks than it would now take hours by jet. But what is almost incredible is that the metamorphosis should have taken place within two generations—even generations covering between them such an unusually long span as do my father's and mine.

If my father saw New York today, a century and a quarter after his birth, he would remember practically nothing from his youth; and indeed it becomes harder and harder for my generation to do so either. First came the brawny Irishmen with their crowbars, knocking down the familiar brownstone and brick, clearing the way for the erection of what to our innocent eyes seemed limestone and marble giants. But these had an even shorter life; soon the acetylene torch was at work on them, slicing through the girders that we saw being hoisted into place only yesterday, while steam shovels rooted up foundations that had seemed laid to last for centuries. Today on these twice-devastated sites arrogant glass and aluminum mammoths await the next destroyer.

The cycle is continuous. When my father came to town as a boy he stayed with his aunt, Mrs. Salter, in a house on the north side of Fourteenth Street, just west of Fifth Avenue. Next door, he remembered, "stood a very pretty little wooden colonial house, painted white, two stories, with a green door and brass knocker, approached by two flights of curving steps. In front of it was a large balm of Gilead tree and a pump then in use, and I have often seen large sows asleep in the gutter on the corner of Fourteenth Street and Fifth Avenue. Indeed, pigs roamed all the streets of the city at that time." Not long afterwards the colonial house was pulled down and the Van Beurens built a fine brownstone town house on the site. In my own childhood it still stood, the last of the old private houses in the block. Then it was replaced by business buildings, for this became a busy shopping neighborhood, with Macy's on the corner of Sixth Avenue and Tiffany's, Brentano's and others nearby on Union Square. Gradually these moved uptown, leaving their premises to a sad medley of "fire-sale" and cut-rate fly-by-nights. Today apartment houses are taking over, each indistinguishable from the next, each a bee's comb of paper-thin cells, what E. E. Cummings called hyperboxes. Soon air conditioners will be dribbling onto the sidewalk; but no moisture will reach the old roots of that balm of Gilead.

When my father was only sixteen his mother died, and thenceforth he was largely on his own. His brothers were kind to him when they remembered, and they saw that his education was continued. In the last years his mother had found Danskammer too expensive to keep up, since she had lost most of her money in the great fire that swept lower New York and ruined the insurance companies in 1835. She therefore had rented Danskammer to Mr. Warren Delano (F.D.R.'s grandfather) and had taken my father to live in the city. She realized he had some artistic talent and arranged that, along with his other studies, he should take lessons in the studio of a Mr. Coe. Though a very mediocre artist indeed, Mr. Coe nevertheless gave him a fondness for painting that eventually led him to what became his life's work.

Now his brothers sent him back to New York, where he boarded alone (except for the company of a red squirrel) at Mrs. Plummer's on the corner of Fifteenth

Street and Union Square, and attended the University Grammar School on the east side of Washington Square, then called the Washington Parade Ground; earlier it had been the Potter's Field for the burial of paupers and criminals, and a place for public executions. In spare time he played with friends in the open pastures and orchards between Seventeenth and Twenty-third streets, skated on a pond near where Forty-second Street crosses Sixth Avenue, and fought the toughs of the neighborhood.

Just before he was ready to go to Trinity College, in Hartford, he decided, with nobody to oppose it and many invitations to make it possible, to spend a winter in Charleston. Theoretically, of course, he was to be busy part of the time with studies, but actually, also of course, he enjoyed to the limit the delightful plantation life of hospitable relatives and friends—shooting snipe on the sedgy banks of the rice fields, quail in the broom grass, deer and wild turkey in the woods, doves among the cornstalks left standing after the ears were picked, woodcock among the bay trees along the lakelike "reserves," duck in the swamps. He was not boastful but could not help recording his best bag—eleven English snipe with thirteen shots. He danced at little parties (he was too young for the Saint Cecilias) and watched the meet at the Charleston Race Course. He detested slavery intensely even when the slaves were, as at Castle Hill and other plantations where he visited, well looked after. Perhaps this was due to the influence of his mother, who had freed the forty slaves she inherited from her father, Colonel John Ward, of Seven Oaks, on John's Island; but essentially, I think, his reaction was instinctive, for all his life he was individualistic and independent in his ideas.

Before Colonel Ward went off to the Revolution he buried his pink Lowestoft china in the sand to hide it from the British who were pillaging the neighborhood after the battle of Stony Ferry; and when the war was over he dug it up again intact (a good part of it is now in my dining room in Tenth Street). His wife, Mary Somersall, is pictured with her mother and grandmother in a portrait which family tradition attributed to Copley; and its distinctive style, particularly the beautiful manner in which the silks are painted, supported that belief. However, the Metropolitan Museum decided when it was there for a loan exhibition that more likely it was by Henry Benbridge, who was painting in this country at the same time as Copley.

With the Charleston winter as background and with no parental guidance it speaks well for my father that he nevertheless entered Trinity College that autumn and began preparing for the Harvard Law School. He had to admit afterwards, however, that sparring, sketching, skating, rowing and riding took up as much of his time at college as did his studies; and when he wrenched his leg badly just after graduation and was threatened with becoming lame he was happy to be advised to take a long sea voyage and thus postpone the next step. So putting aside his letters of introduction to Mr. Longfellow and Dr. Theophilus Parsons, dean of the Law School, he set sail in November 1858 in a little clipper-built craft of three hundred tons, the *Celestia*, bound for Sicily. The storms weathered before they reached Madeira, the sercial, bual and malmsey drunk there with hospitable Mr. Cossart, the wine merchant, the adventure of being run down thereafter by a large steamer, the *Great Britain,* but sticking by the *Celestia* till she limped into Gibraltar, where another bark was found that eventually made Messina—this is a tale already told.* From Sicily he went on to Rome in January 1859.

Happily there was no railway in those days, so from the port of Civitavecchia he travelled up to Rome by diligence. It must have been a heavenly way to reach Rome for the first (or any) time, above all for an embryo artist.

That first morning [he wrote afterwards] was one to be remembered, delicious as only an Italian winter's day can be; under a soft haze the landscape melted away in almost imperceptible folds and tones, in varied graduations and shades of opalescent and silvery color, touched here and there by a line of the first fresh green of the wheat-fields or a faint glistening spot of water. All was remote and solemn. In the distance, the turrets of an old castle of Julius the Second peered through shadowy groves of stone-pines above vast tan-colored marshes. . . .

So our day passed. Suddenly our vetturino, with a crack of the whip, shouted "Ecco Roma!" and we saw shining in the extreme distance, like a great pearl, as Story calls it, that grew and grew, the splendid dome of St. Peter's. . . . Our horses dashed through a tall archway directly from the quiet Campagna into the Square of San Pietro, and there was the honey-colored façade of Bramante's basilica embraced by its grand colonnades, and the Egyptian obelisk flanked by the noble fountains, flinging high their spray that drifted across the square in silvery clouds.

* *Day Before Yesterday,* by Maitland Armstrong. New York: Scribner's, 1920, Chapter VI.

My first childhood sight of that dome, nearly fifty years later, was from our bedroom at the Hotel Eden, across the pines, almonds and Judas trees of the Villa Medici. It was not so small as when Papa first saw it gleaming afar across the Campagna, but it nevertheless fitted neatly into the very center of the window. I was sad when that same day we moved for economy's sake to a smaller hotel opposite the Palazzo Borghese.

This trip of my father's in 1859 did not attempt the whole Grand Tour of Europe then prescribed as part of a young man's education, but it was enough to change the course of his life (and the lives of his children) by developing interests that compelled him to become an artist instead of going on with the law. It is worth a paragraph, perhaps, to indicate a few of the sights that attracted the interest of a young American visiting Europe for the first time a century ago.

After Rome came Florence (at carnival time) and Bologna (visited partly in order to see the Guido Renis there; he confessed that at twenty-three he had had what he called "a terrible liking" for Guido); Venice (where in compensation for his taste for Guido his diary glowingly describes the majestic Colleoni); and Paris (where he saw the Empress Eugenie, crying, driving with Louis Napoleon on his way to his great victories at Solferino and Magenta). In London he was incensed to find Turners hung next to Claude Lorrains, with which, to his mind, they could not stand comparison, "notwithstanding Mr. Ruskin," and where he liked the Hogarths but also the Landseers (he hoped later this had been because he was a dog lover); he also saw Charles Kean in *Henry V*, heard Spurgeon, unctuous and oily, attended

Derby Day at Epsom, and went out to Eton where he watched boys playing cricket, rowing, bird nesting, fishing and shooting, and wrote in his diary, "It seems worth while to go to a school like that."

From London he went on to visit his godfather, David Maitland, at his place in Kirkcudbrightshire, a stone house, in the midst of gardens enriched with Cherokee roses brought home by Mr. Maitland when he returned from making a fortune in New York, and surrounded by a thousand acres of half-moorland farm through which ran the River Dee. It was not the shooting season, but he could sketch, and did. In Dumfriesshire he drew ruined Gilnockie Castle, the home of a much-sung forbear, the Border Chieftain Johnny Armstrong. As the old chronicle says: "The Armestrongges of Liddersdaill had repoorted presumptuously that they woode not be ordoured, naither by the king of Scottes thair soveraine lorde nor by the king of England, but after suche maner as thaire faders had used afore Thayme." This was too much; Johnny and his men were taken by a ruse and hanged. But, say the ballads, the leaves withered and no tree has grown since on the sandy Caerlanrig plateau.

After this taste of Europe my father found it hard to settle down to studying law in Judge Kent's office in New York, and soon after his marriage he seized with alacrity the chance to go back to Rome as consul to the Papal States. This was in 1869. He and my mother had the upper part of the Palazzo Zuccari on the Via Sistina running through to the Via Gregoriana, a glorious situation overlooking the Piazza di Spagna with St. Peter's in the middle distance and the hills of shifting light and color beyond. The work as consul was far from onerous;

a large part of it seems to have consisted of telling most visiting Americans that they could not be received in private audience by the Pope, Pio Nono, or instructing the vice-consul to arrange for the presentation of those who could be. This left him plenty of time to sketch, hunt on the Campagna, buy *roba di Roma* to the extent that his meager resources allowed, and enjoy the intellectual and artistic amenities of a Roman society that was more sober in those days, and certainly not less cultivated, than it became a generation or two later.

The State Department being under the fortunate impression that Rome was insupportable in hot weather, the family spent the summers in the north; by this time it included, besides my eldest sister Margaret, my sister Helen, born in Florence because of the same fear of the Roman climate and the belief that Florence would be healthier. For the first part of the summer of 1870 they had been at a hotel on Monte Generoso (there was no funicular then, so they ascended on horseback, the nurse carrying the littlest baby in her arms, each trunk on a separate mule), and in August of that year, a month memorable in Italian history, they were settled at Bellagio. Then came word that Victor Emmanuel's troops were approaching Rome, and my father set out for there at once. Three days' travel, the last twenty-five miles by box wagon, brought him at evening to the old Nomentano bridge; the tents of the Italian army, sixty thousand strong, dotted the hills and cavalry were moving about on the plain. He got through the Papal guards at the Porto Pia to find the city hushed and empty of almost all foreigners. Early on September 20 heavy cannonading began, and towards noon my father walked in the direction of the Porto Pia, passing on the way the grounds of the Villa Buonaparte where the Italians had breached the wall and killed several Papal Zouaves. Beyond, he came upon the main body of the Zouaves, disarmed and disheveled, marching two by two between files of Italian *Bersaglieri* who spat at them and thumped their toes with the butts of their guns. By evening the city had erupted with Italian flags, soldiers were everywhere, horses were tethered in all the squares, and the crowds went wild as though there had been a real war and a real battle. I think, in all, seven Zouaves were killed.

Overnight, Rome left the Middle Ages and Roman society changed from "black" to "white." My father had less to do now with the Papal Secretary of State, Cardinal Antonelli, but very much to do with the new Italian Foreign Minister, Visconti-Venosta. Among the scraps of reminiscence that I picked up later about his busy life, there was none of political importance to compare in interest for me with the tale of one unimportant incident. It had to do with an affair, as it used to be called in novels, of honor. He was challenged to a duel.

This is how it came about. There was to be a fancy-dress ball at which members of the royal family were to be present, organized for charity by the foreign colony. The committee (my father was treasurer) had been advised from the Quirinal that several unsavory characters on the fringes of Roman society should not be invited. One was a certain Count Ajasso, a professional duellist, a bully, a gambler, with a wife conspicuous in pursuits which could hardly be cited as a reason for not issuing the couple an invitation. Thus when

Count Ajasso asked for tickets my father had to tell him that none were available and, when pressed, added that he did not feel obliged to give any reason. The next day three visiting cards bearing the names and coronets of three Italian officers (rumored to be deeply in debt to the count) were handed in at my father's house. They informed him that they were Ajasso's seconds, that he demanded tickets, an apology or a reason for refusing them, with the further alternative that my father name his seconds for a duel. All these he declined, saying that a duel was out of the question, not only because he was his government's representative in Rome but also because duelling was against the law and custom of the United States. That evening at the opera the count's friends came up to another member of the committee, Frederic Crowninshield, informed him that the count would cane Mr. Armstrong in the street, and what would he do then? The reply that doubtless he would defend himself "in the usual American fashion" was cryptic, suggesting perhaps revolvers and bowie knives; and the affair seemed to lapse. Then one day my father met Ajasso on the Spanish Steps.

"I was walking home after a ride," he wrote, "and had started up the left flight of steps when, glancing up, I saw Ajasso at the top at the right. So I retraced my steps and went up the right side. I hoped that the caning was about to begin, as he had a stick in his hand, and I shifted my riding-crop from my left hand to my right and swung it thoughtfully. But it was not to be—a glare was his only revenge. A year later he was killed in a duel."

I always regretted, of course, that the duel had not

been fought and that my father had not run the miscreant count through (how, since he had never fenced, I didn't stop to consider). But when I went to Rome as a child I took satisfaction in climbing the Spanish Steps on the right-hand side and choosing the spot where my father had swung his riding crop against his boot and the abashed count had passed him by.

I can't resist adding one more of my father's stories. While Saint-Gaudens was modeling a bust of General Sherman he also was at work on a bas-relief of Robert Louis Stevenson. He mentioned to Sherman that he would like to introduce Stevenson to him.

"Was he one of my boys?" the general asked.

"No," replied Saint-Gaudens. "He's a celebrated writer, the author of *Dr. Jekyll and Mr. Hyde.*"

"Then he's no fool," said the general.

The next morning when Stevenson came in for a sitting Saint-Gaudens introduced them.

"Glad to meet you, sir!" said the general. "Were you one of my boys?"

After the unification of Italy my father was promoted to be consul general. This increased his duties greatly; and when it began to be rumored that he might be named minister, replacing Mr. Marsh, who resided in Florence, he realized that if he were to pursue a serious career as an artist and make enough of a living to bring up his children (though he probably did not visualize that there would be seven of them), he had best return home without more delay. It turned out that he was the last official to represent the United States government at the Vatican. In 1939 President Roosevelt appointed Myron Taylor as his personal representative there, and

President Truman continued the appointment; but there has been no official representative since my father left in 1872. His intention was to divide his time between painting and growing fruit at Danskammer, imagining, probably, that the latter would provide the wherewithal to make the former possible.

Gradually he began working more and more in stained glass. He and his friend La Farge developed new techniques in opalescent glass, sometimes "plating" their windows with as many as three or four thicknesses, one on top of the other, thereby giving them depth and glorious color. In this they differed from the windows later on manufactured by commercial artisans for churches all across the country which gave "American glass" such a bad name. When he became too busy to look after the three thousand peach trees and several acres of grapes at Danskammer, he bought the house in Tenth Street, cut down on farming and spent only the summers on the River. Such was the order of things when I was added to the family.

IV

*I have memory of a place and a magical time
in which the Sun and the Moon were larger and
brighter than now.*

—LAFCADIO HEARN, "Out of the East"

A LANE RAN UPHILL FROM THE MAIN ROAD TO THE
Danskammer farm. First it passed over a small stream,
full the year round of swaying watercress, under swift-
flowing water in summer, under fringes of ice in winter.
The red-brick bridge had a stone coping which the sun
warmed pleasantly for sitting on in autumn. Once over
the bridge, the lane turned sharply upwards, passed over
two "thank-you-mams" and continued at a gentler grade
between low stone walls and through red cedars, butternuts and hickories. It was actually about half a mile, I
suppose, but seemed more because of the diversions
along the way—anise, with a lovely licoricy taste, sassa-
fras roots to grub up and wintergreen leaves to chew if
you liked wintergreen. In early spring the lady's-slippers
made spots of pink and yellow in the sunny open woods.
Where the land levelled out, the corn and hay fields
began; beyond on the left were the red barns and stable

and, further on, to the right, the garden and orchard.

The house, at the top of a long slope down to the River, had begun as a farmhouse; my father kept it as his part of his mother's property, and when he returned from Rome he began doing it over and enlarging it bit by bit. His architect friends White and McKim came there often, and he had trouble resisting their alluring plans for this or that large addition. He said later, when it was hard to remember that tiles and Morris wallpapers and chintzes had ever been considered novel and beautiful, that there had been too much of the aesthetic in his youthful decorations; but he still believed, with Oscar Wilde, that sunflowers and lilies were better than black walnut and green rep.

I was christened nearby, in the little church at Marlborough built by my grandmother (my brother Noel was disappointed when he learnt this did not mean she had built it *with her own hands*). My Uncle Gov had been told that I was to be named Gouverneur after him, and on that premise he went to the ceremony, a concession on his part since he had not been inside a church for thirty or forty years. On the drive up to Marlborough my mother changed her mind and decided to name me after a favorite uncle of hers who had just died. Uncle Gov heard the news only when the clergyman reached the place in the service "Name this child." He felt defrauded on two counts, the wrong name, and having been inveigled into church on false pretenses.

None of my family had the strength of character to keep a diary for long, but Marion persevered through most of one winter at Danskammer; it was the beginning of 1895, she was fourteen, Noel was twelve and I was not yet two. The two things she recorded most consistently were, first, the number of books she read (at least one every two or three days, not short books either, but *Old Mortality, Northanger Abbey, The Master of Ballantrae* and such); and, second, the number of skunks shot or trapped by Noel (he was in the fur business, and an entry in May, at the end of the season, shows it was profitable: "Noel sold all his skunk skins for $2.50"). I appear occasionally as a nuisance: "Baby bothered and blotted this" or "Ham poured water on the clean clothes." Sometimes she wrote commiseratingly: "Ham sat down in a pail of cold water." Sometimes admiringly: "Mamma left the baby alone a minute to go for something, she came back and he had got the cornpopper and box of corn, put some in, shut it, held it over the fire and was saying, Pop, pop." She recorded my first full sentence, already a demand, a month before my second birthday: "More tea for baby."

The hillside from the house down to the River was a vineyard; in the season of grapes the whole countryside up to Marlborough and beyond was sweet with their smell. Papa disdained Concords. There were little Delawares for eating, pink and very sweet, and Catawbas to be packed and shipped off to market; but he held back enough to make a hundred or so bottles of wine for his fruit punches. There was every other sort of fruit, too—strawberries, eaten straight from the patch, warm and a little dusty, never washed; muskmelons, also particularly sweet when warm; cherries, plums and peaches; more currants and gooseberries than could be made into jellies and jams; quinces with furry cheeks; Seckel pears, not even distant relatives to the stony ob-

œ *34*

jects masquerading under the name in city groceries ("never pick them; only the ones on the ground are good"); conical Porter summer apples, enormous smooth King apples on two trees that stood by themselves, and last of all the winter apples, Northern Spys and Baldwins.

My mother had been run away with so often in the course of years in the country that she had developed a real aversion to horses and only used them as a necessity, never for pleasure. My sisters liked riding, but less well, Helen told me later, than my father thought they did. The trouble was probably the clothes: thick cloth habits, very tight, padded on the shoulders, linen collars and cuffs, hard hats, either top hats or derbys, wadded inside, long covert cloth trousers under the skirts, and dogskin gloves. They were expected to keep the buttons down the front of their habits straight and in line with the horse's mane. On a broiling Hudson River afternoon Margaret and Helen were good sports, I think, even to say they enjoyed it. Of course the farm also had cows and chickens and a pigsty overflowing with a recumbent sow and a row of tugging piglets.

All this was run by a wonderful farmer whom I revered and loved, Alexander, a tall, spare, dignified, gentle Scotch-Irishman with a red beard, and his Irish helper, James Hannigan, bald and with a knobbly chin covered with a deep stubble all week and shining with a dark metallic blue on Sundays. Regardless of weather, Hannigan wore a red flannel shirt, a thick cloth waistcoat and an old derby hat. One of Alexander's daughters, Mamie, an intelligent and beautiful girl, came as my nurse when she was fifteen or sixteen; she practically

35

brought me up, and I adored and usually obeyed her. Alexander took me on his lap while ploughing or haying or mowing the lawn, and let me hold the reins. When the corn was being stacked we might find a nest of tiny field mice, pink-nosed and blind, which I'd try to keep alive by feeding with an eyedropper. When, as happened quite often, the plough turned up an arrowhead, sometimes of translucent white quartz, more often of black flint, I jumped down for it. This naturally set me to imagining Indians appearing with war whoops from behind the red barn; but the quiet swishing of the horses' tails as Alexander calmly waited for me to climb back into his lap made it too difficult. I tried to help along the farm's economy by collecting in my cart along the driveway the valuable product which I saw being spread in the garden. This was the only thing I did of which Alexander ever disapproved.

Despite everyone's efforts the farm always ran at a loss, but by working hard on the days he was in New York my father was able to afford it. Before my time, he had experimented with imported Hampshire Downs, the first sheep of this kind seen in this part of the Hudson Valley; but they were killed by dogs. He also tried turkeys, but they were always getting lost or dying after a wetting in a thunderstorm; and though his game fowl took prizes they were really a fad. The chickens were profitable, but only after he gave up feeding them, in accordance with directions in a French book, on onion grass chopped up in curds and claret; in spite of, or because of, this expensive diet, many of them died of the "gapes," but the survivors multiplied on a more conventional American menu. When I was very small

the peaches were still flourishing, and I watched dis-
believingly as great baskets of them were piled high on
a wagon drawn by four horses to catch the night boat at
Marlborough. Were there really enough people in the
city to eat all those peaches?

Above the barns to the north was Beacon Hill, covered with cedars and sumac, the abode of copperheads
and red foxes, for which Noel set traps. Once my father
forced Saint-Gaudens to climb to the top and admire
the broad view down the River to the other Beacon Hill
near Fishkill, another link in the signal chain used by
the Iroquois and later by their allies the British during
the Revolution. Saint-Gaudens, who didn't care about
exercise, retaliated by telling of a Frenchman forced
into a similar expedition who replied to the question
whether he didn't love the beauties of nature, "Moi, je
les abhorre." I heard the story because even in my time
"Moi, je les abhorre" was a family way of replying to
saccharin remarks about sunsets and red maples and
such.

Below Beacon Hill was Collie Hook, swampy and
cool even in summer, and to the south Danskammer
Point pushed further out into the River; a little lighthouse had been built there after a steamer ran ashore
and broke off the big flat rock where Hudson's Indians
had danced. "Bumboats," evading the local liquor laws,
sometimes came stealthily into the cove, enticing farm-
hands or brickyard laborers to row out for a bottle of
gin. I didn't understand why they came only at twilight
and usually slunk away quickly, but the whole operation
was sinister and brought to mind pirates. Bittersweet
grew in dense tangles all over the Point, and where it

had twisted itself deeply into the bark of a sapling my brother Noel would cut me a walking stick so that I could imagine myself Mercury with his rod of twined serpents.

One among my recollections at Danskammer is not quite sure; perhaps it is only a fantasy of something dreadful that might have happened. It is a summer day, just after lunch; we have waved our napkins at the Day Line boat going up to Albany and been saluted in return by the usual puffs of smoke and the whistle—a long and two shorts—that followed lazily. Now Mamma is pouring coffee for some friends on the lawn, and I am rashly allowed to hand around the little cups. I still see and feel how I plunge into old Mr. Choate's lap, planting the cup against his stomach and aware with horror of the hot contents trickling down my bare legs, just as I knew without daring to look that it was trickling down his linen waistcoat.

Perhaps my doubt whether this fearful scene really occurred was simply the result of my sister Marion's teasing about my eagerness to know and remember things that I didn't. I would go to any length of unveracity in order not to be left out.

"Do you remember the parrot at Danskammer?"

"Yes," I'd reply without hesitation.

"What color?"

"Well, greenish mainly."

Of course there never had been a parrot of any color. But I think Marion was going too far, indeed made it all up, about the time the Bishop came to lunch after preaching one Sunday in the Marlborough Church. I had been told to be on my particularly good behavior.

As she related it with appropriate unction, I turned to the Bishop after grace, trying hard:

"Please pass the butter, for Jesus Christ's sake."

Neither of the Day boats, the *Albany* and the *New York,* though faithful with their salutes, was such a favorite as the svelte *Mary Powell,* with her walking beam and foaming side paddles, the fastest boat on the River. (My family wrote "River" with a capital letter, as if there were no other stream in the world.) The reputation of the *Mary Powell* as a speedy lady was widespread. Long after she had gone to the scrap heap, evidence of it still survived carved into one of the tables in the old "Nass" at Princeton, where among the tangled names of undergraduates of the nineties, now past carousing, MARY POWELL, in capital letters, occupied a central place, reminder of a toast to both elegance and speed.

Mr. Choate's visit to Danskammer may have been in return for one of those my father used to make to Stockbridge and other places within a riding radius of three or four days. Usually on these trips he would stop overnight with friends, but once in Stockbridge he put up at the Red Lion Inn, where the waitress went round at dinner asking the guests, "Pie or puddin'?"

"What kind of pie?" my father inquired.

"Lost your chance," she said and passed on.

"Lost your chance" became a stock answer in our impatient family to anyone who delayed more than a split second in making even a hard choice.

The part of the Danskammer house that had once been a farm cottage was over two hundred years old. The new part was built with higher ceilings, with the result that nothing inside was on the same level. You entered the hall by a Dutch door, divided across the middle so that the upper half let in air and light while the lower half kept out the dogs. To the right was the library, with a Franklin stove and bookshelves to the ceilings. The dining room fireplace was surrounded with the same set of blue-and-white Dutch tiles that Scrooge had in his bedroom, but instead of a measly fire hardly big enough to warm Scrooge's gruel there was always a blaze of big logs in chilly weather. The sideboard was old American, in which the local carpenter, Marcus D. Kelly, had built extra shelves. He had been named for the Marquis de Lafayette, which explains why he didn't know what the middle initial stood for. The heating system functioned in only the new part of the house, and not very robustly at that. There was, of course, no electric light. Water came from a hand pump in the kitchen, beside the door to the "cold pantry" where the preserves and vegetables were stored. It all sounds uncomfortable but wasn't.

The best room, to my mind, was the nursery, which I was the last in line to inherit. On autumn evenings Mamie would put a round green tin tub close in front of the Franklin stove; it was not too high to step into but deep enough to float the necessary toys. All around the room, at the height of a child's eye, ran a frieze of Walter Crane pictures, the "Black Dwarf," "Beauty and the Beast," "La Belle Etoile" and all the rest, mysterious but familiar enough not to be eerie as the light from the stove flickered low before you went to sleep.

In my time, my father was at Danskammer too irregularly to continue as warden at the Marlborough Church. Formerly he had acted for it in almost every capacity.

He read the lessons, and when the rector was away, or in intervals when he was looking for a new one, he read the service too and gave the sermon. When I asked how he had managed the sermon, Helen said it was generally one by Canon Farrar—"and even better than the original, because he left out all the doctrinal parts and left in all the poetry and quotations." Once when there was a vacancy, Papa sent Helen and my brother Maitland down to see whether the curate at St. Paul's Chapel in New York might do. She was twenty-four, Maitland was twenty. When this unusual delegation approached the curate at the door after the service he must have been considerably surprised. Helen couldn't remember whether they thought he would "do," or whether if so he had accepted.

Helen described the Marlborough Church in those days as dismal—"a black walnut altar; over it a window of Faith, a long way after Reynolds; no hangings, no flowers, no ornaments until Aunt Mattie (Uncle Harry's wife) gave two silver vases which however usually remained empty; a little red cloth hanging from the lectern, always crooked; the Rector in too short a surplice and no cassock."

"We were always late," she remembered. "Mamma didn't like to be coerced by Time and Papa was always busy at something up to the last minute."

In the pew in front sat a large old lady in the venerable clothes of her youth—bustles, overskirts and bonnets with streamers. She was redolent of St. Jacob's oil, supposedly potent against rheumatism, and Papa had to wear a marigold in his buttonhole and pinch it at intervals to drown the smell.

On the way to church we passed by Uncle Harry's place, the Eckhert Farm, part of a grant of land by Queen Anne to Wolfert Eckhert (who also built Wolfert's Roost, the house where Washington Irving lived after changing the name to Sunnyside). This was the oldest house in the neighborhood, built originally as a blockhouse with enormously thick walls for defense against the Indians. Uncle Harry was the most adventurous of my uncles. I remember him as wiry and brisk, but shrunk from the erect and defiant figure shown in daguerreotypes. He had knocked all about the world, first as a cabin boy in a clipper bound for Hong Kong under the command of the notorious Bob Waterman (later tried for murdering a sailor); then, after an interval studying first the law and then medicine, he became a forty-niner. He joined French's Expedition in Galveston, and when that dispersed in dissention he bought a horse and set out to ride alone to California, passing by the site of the present El Paso and swimming his horse across the Colorado. In the mining camp (he told my father, who told me, for I was always asking questions beginning *who, why* and *when?*) he officiated at funerals, for he was the only one with a prayer book, and once he amputated a man's leg, for which, since it turned out a success, he was paid $500 in raw gold. He also told my father that he had seen a barkeeper take hold of a man who wouldn't pay for his drinks, put his head on the counter and cut his throat with the knife he used for slicing lemons. Adventures behind him, he now lived quietly (and soberly) with his wife, broken in spirit since his only child, a little girl, had been drowned in the brook in front of the house.

The summer of 1898—the year of the Spanish-American War—was the first that my family spent entirely away from Danskammer. Brickyards were changing the neighborhood. Our farm was intact but not unaffected. The hillsides to the south were being gnawed away; taverns had sprung up; and workmen, after stops at one or more of them, lay sprawled of an evening by the roadside. In a few years the useful red clay around the old Danskammer house would be consumed almost to the foundations, leaving the massive columns standing bleakly on a naked peninsula above gullies of mud and sand where green woods, gardens and lawns had sloped down to the River. Later the portico was taken to pieces and carted off to be rebuilt elsewhere, after F.D.R.'s uncle, Fred Delano, who loved the neighborhood, had failed in his scheme to move the house to Washington to serve as a "state house" for New York congressmen and visiting officials.

This summer my father took a cottage on Fishers Island, where the guns of Fort Wright fired at all hours, only for practice, of course, although there were constant rumors that hostile ships had been sighted here, there and everywhere until the main Spanish fleet was sunk in the Battle of Santiago. It was a short war, with not many casualties, and for the rest not too hard on anyone except the boys who got malaria or were poisoned by the War Department's "embalmed beef." What I noticed more than the guns of Fort Wright were the hares that went bounding away through the dunes as we drove to Isabella Beach. They looked almost as large as the horses. Would the carriage turn over if one leapt in? There was a hotel near the landing, the Mansion

House, with rows of creaking rockers on the long piaz-
zas; apart from that, two or three cottages, a small store
or two and a few fishermen's houses the island was
empty and beautiful. The Ferguson family, who owned
most of the island and rented us our small cottage, had
a Japanese butler who made me a red box kite and
showed me how to fly it. In a good wind it would roll
me across the lawn until I landed in a heap against the
hedge.

My eldest brother, Maitland, had joined the Philadelphia City Troop and by fall was in Puerto Rico, whence
he returned without wounds or glory but with chronic
catarrh and slightly deaf. It was a sad sequel to the
proud day when we had hung out a flag in Tenth Street
and gathered on the stoop to see him off in uniform. In
a commemorative snapshot the top of my head just
shows above the railing. The general opinion was that
Maitland was the good-looking male member of the
family; but I much preferred the looks of Noel, perhaps
because though nearer my age he was still enough older
to be a hero to me in every respect—six feet one, modest,
quiet (the only reticent member of the family), with
muscles of iron, capable of everything, especially anything to be done with one's hands and above all anything to be done outdoors: "tender and true."

When my father came for weekends at Fishers Island,
or at North Hatley, the Quebec village where we spent
summers later, he always had armfuls of presents—hard
candy for me, or fireworks if it was just before the
Fourth, peaches or pears for Helen, who missed the
Danskammer fruit, a couple of new novels by Edith
Wharton or Henry James, and a box of Huyler's "for

everybody." This summer, I remember, he brought me a shallow oblong box with the battleship *Maine* painted inside on the bottom—or rather, on the false bottom, for there was room underneath for a fuse to be attached, with just the end sticking conveniently out near some dusky-hued desperadoes on the shore who were making as though to light it. When you actually did light the fuse it sputtered slowly toward the battleship, riding majestically on a bright blue ocean, with the stars and stripes floating at the stern, half as large again as the whole ship. Then came a lovely fizz and a small puff of smoke, betokening the end of the *Maine*. However, the picture remained, and as a package of spare fuses was provided you could astound or, you hoped, frighten members of the family or visitors over and over again. A similar game based on the double-bottom principle was concerned with sending McGinty to the bottom of the sea, in accordance with a song of the day, but just how that operation was performed I can't recall.

The culmination of the war, for New York at any rate, was the Dewey parade, which involved putting up a big white plaster and papier-mâché arch and a series of pylons on Fifth Avenue at Madison Square. The intention was to perpetuate them later in marble, but instead they disintegrated gradually along with Dewey's fame, and finally when they were a sooty grey they were carted away and never replaced. At first, everyone was proud of the victory, but later became incensed when the fever-stricken and food-poisoned soldiers began reaching home and told of the incredible mismanagement in the army commissariat and medical corps. It was due to the scandals of that day and the subsequent reforms that those of us who were in the army in a later war were not fed putrefied bully beef and had a competent medical corps. Perhaps, as I never got close to a front line, I have missed seeing army operations at their efficient best. In my limited view, however, it has always seemed fortunate that when one's army fights a war its antagonist is another army, often with the same glorious merits but also with the same stubborn defects; if your army were up against any other sort of organization than another army it would be in real trouble.

After the Fishers Island summer we went back to Danskammer for only a few weeks in spring and autumn. The nursery was given over to visitors now and I had a snug little room overlooking the River, down two steps from my parents' room and up one from the hall. From where I lay in bed the branches made a sharp black pattern against the moonglade on the River, and on misty nights the lighthouse bell came through muffled, as from a great distance. By then I was seven or eight, and Helen was reading and rereading the *Morte d'Arthur* to me from a favorite little four-volume edition illustrated by Aubrey Beardsley. The bare branches outside my window twisted easily into pictures as intricate as Beardsley's. It took practically no imagination at all to see through the bare autumn branches Merlin half-hiding in his dark forest or the shadowy form of Gawain the parfait knight.

Each trip up and down the River on the West Shore Railroad was a new experience. I kept careful records in a small notebook of the times of arrival and departure at all the stations—Haverstraw, Stony Point, Tompkins Cove, Iona Island. Each name as sung out by the conductor had its own melody. When we were on time my pride was at least equal to the engineer's, and probably I felt a more keen sense of responsibility when we were late. The hawker who came through the train sold Ridley's Broken Candy in paper cornucopias. My father remembered that his godfather, Mr. David Maitland, used to bring this same sort of candy as his invariable present when he came to the old Danskammer about 1840. Names had changed in the intervening sixty years but not the colors and flavors—pink cinnamon, striped wintergreen, white vanilla, clear lemon, and a deceivingly lemon-appearing variety that disgustingly turned out to be clove. Another sixty years have obliterated both name (so far as I know) and product, indeed have come close to obliterating the West Shore Railroad.

V

I get quickly tired of hearing other people giving information without help from me.

—STELLA BENSON, "This Is the End"

ONE ADVANTAGE OF BEING THE YOUNGEST OF A big family is that if ever your parents were inclined to fuss they by now have tired of it. Mine, I think, took all their children fairly calmly, without preconceived fads or fancies about education. My older sisters grew up with tastes, and soon with occupations, in line with my father's; by the time they were eighteen and nineteen they were selling their drawings and covers to *Harper's* and *Scribner's,* concealing the fact that they were girls, for female talent was then at a discount. This meant that the main stream of family activity and talk was artistic. The second group of children—Marion and Noel, with me tagging along as an afterthought—were different. But by their time the family pattern was set and they fitted into it as best they could or went their own ways outside it. What Marion's was not was plain from her unhappy remark, echo of Longfellow, "Art is so long."

It must not be supposed that there were no restraints in Tenth Street, no family rules; there were, and they were observed as a matter of course. There was church and there was Sunday school beforehand. Sunday afternoons were sedate; games were not played, not even Avilude and Ferelude, an instructive card game miraculously surviving from my grandparents' time. (The aim was to match up a family of birds or animals—hence the erudite name. The anteater was especially repulsive and I always tried for a set that didn't need him.) On Sundays and for parties the usual blue serge gave way to sailor suits of linen or another less scratchy material, some of them with long trousers with square flaps which buttoned confusingly across the front (these came from Peter Robinson in London and were hand-me-downs from cousins who had outgrown them). Later when obligatory dress became the short jacket, long trousers and turnover collar of an Eton suit the burden was terrific but was borne as something predestined. You were supposed to show more consideration of the feelings of servants, who could not reply to rudeness in kind, than of your friends. You were to stand up and speak to visitors. You were to be on time for meals, "sit up," not put your elbows on the table (even in summer for corn), chew with your mouth closed and not scrape your plate. The rule about being on time held even at lunch when my father often arrived late from his studio on Washington Square or from the glass shop.

Lunch generally was large and noisy, two or three friends probably having dropped in to sit with my sisters while they finished their work in the studio upstairs.

My father would come in hurriedly, still perhaps with a smudge of paint on his chin, hungry and talkative, wanting a change from what he had been thinking and doing. All the others were talkative too, often simultaneously; they seemed to be satisfied to get off whatever was on their minds whether or not anybody was paying proper attention. Conversation in the family was bubbling, rather than the sort in which people take turns clearing their throat to get attention for a story. Contributing to this spontaneity was an engaging attitude revealed by a remark of Margaret's which has now passed into the folklore of quotations: "How do I know what I think till I hear what I say?" I repeated it often, and in due time began hearing it quoted back to me; which is how bons mots become chestnuts. To the prevailing disorder I contributed my share, judging by a repeated plea of Marion's to which I paid no attention: "Mamma, isn't there *any* way of keeping Hamilton from talking?" (She usually called me Ham, but Hamilton when she was exasperated.) Despite all this the family talk was good talk, whether everyone listened to everybody or not; and as it ranged over everything under the sun, from "Nude Descending a Staircase" to women's suffrage, I got a good deal of my education there.

As a family we were not mechanically minded (except Noel) and were hopeless at mathematics (except Margaret). Margaret could do accounts, and had to, because Mamma worried so if she did them. Fortunately, Papa had a bookkeeper at his office, but he had trouble with his personal checkbook, where the balance at the end of the month never agreed with that reported by the bank. I inherited the same weakness; indeed, I never really mastered the multiplication table to the point where I knew it beyond any shadow of a doubt. Today I still am so unconfident when, for instance, I put down 9×9 as 81 that I find myself automatically checking in the back of my mind (a misnomer evidently in this connection)—yes, 9×10 is 90, and this less 9 is indeed 81.

My father could do the most delicate things with a pencil or brush, could make anything grow in a garden and had the lightest of hands on a bridle, but when faced with some odd job was likely to hit on an ingenious but impractical way of solving it. He did not swear. When I heard him mutter "Botheration!" I knew that some little thing had gone wrong, the *passe partout* around a sketch had lost its stickum or the glue wasn't holding together a broken majolica jar. "Confound it!" did for bigger mishaps, as when a nail came out and a picture fell with a clatter. When he said "Thunderation!" I knew he had pierced his thumb with a tack or hit it with a hammer when driving a garden stake. In extremis, "Damnation!" could be heard, the emphasis on the second syllable, but very much under his breath.

The house was particularly crowded in the holidays when my older brothers were home from school or college. Then Noel slept on a cot in one corner of the studio. A boxing bag was suspended directly over his head. When he and his friends wanted to use it—fists, elbows and foreheads alternating in a rapid rat-tat-tat —the cot would be pushed aside. Between holidays the crinkled brown leather hung limply from the ceiling. As Papa had been brought up in a day when the art of self-defense was important he had taught Maitland and Noel to spar as a matter of course, and one of the earliest pieces of practical information he imparted to me was that if I got into a fight I must remember to keep my thumb crooked along the side of my knuckles, not sticking up or folded inside. He evidently considered the information so universally applicable that he must even had imparted it to my older sisters, though they were slight in build and not combative, for I once heard Helen passing the instructions along to my young daughter.

The departure of Noel and his neighborhood friends for boarding school put an end to the wild bicycle hockey that had been played up and down Tenth Street, Fifth Avenue one goal, Sixth Avenue the other. Spills were innumerable, but however dire the need for replacements Marion was the only girl allowed to join in. In the holidays, now, there was talk of the good old days when Tenth Street had been really Tenth Street; but it was only talk, for they all were too busy with other things to get out their bicycles. As for me, I had no bicycle and was more than content with my roller skates.

Marion considered me a pest, and properly. My flow of questions was inexhaustible and I was always popping up where not wanted. If there seemed to be a pause when she was sitting with some admirer in the parlor I would part the curtains and helpfully start making conversation. "Reddy" Choate, who had very long legs, had his own way of getting rid of me; with a false display of friendship he would inveigle me close, catch me between the knees, then squeeze and squeeze (his face all the time out of reach of my fists) until I wriggled loose and escaped.

When I was spanked it was for doing something which was deliberately disobedient, such as locking myself in the bathroom to avoid taking citrate of magnesia, which sends bubbles up your nose. The family medicine chest was much simpler in those days, and I can remember precisely the look and taste of its contents. There were sweet spirits of nitre to reduce fever and Copenhagen cherry brandy to restore your strength afterwards. For stomach aches there was paregoric, most delicious, or perhaps a few drops of brandy on a lump of sugar. I still judge brandy by whether or not it tastes the way I remember brandy did then. For malaria, there was Powers and Weightman's quinine, a wafer that came folded up in a little paper package; it was swallowed with water, but sometimes stuck. Citrate of magnesia I would go to any lengths to avoid. The time I locked myself into the bathroom I resolved to stay there "forever." After an eternity, probably half an hour, I emerged and of course had to swallow the stuff, bubbles or no bubbles, and have a spanking as well.

Though I was enchanted with Miss Lane's school there was one activity indirectly connected with it which I found embarrassing. This was singing class, held at the Beekmans', a wide brownstone house on Fifth Avenue near Twelfth Street. Occasionally I went to play with the Beekman sisters in the vast dimly-lit attic, full of all sorts of odds and ends, old coat racks with antler pegs, tall canes two generations at least out of fashion, mahogany washstands, flowered slop pails and chamber pots in piles, large-busted dressmaker dummies and trunkfuls of the dresses that had once been draped across them, high chairs for babies babies no longer, bundles of faded damask curtains, japanned boxes of receipted bills for food long eaten, services long rendered—every sort of thing outworn or forgotten or replaced by something more admired, afterwards to be replaced no doubt by something better or at any rate newer. These accumulations made the attic ideal for dress-up games or playing at housekeeping. The only drawback was that you couldn't tell ghost stories in a place so ghostly.

I thought of the attic longingly when at ages ranging from five or six to eight or nine we assembled twenty strong around the piano in the drawing room downstairs and obediently sang in uncertain treble "Little John, Bottle John lived on a hill" or "Sweet and low, sweet and low, wind of the western sea," drawing out the final "sleeps" in an orgy of up-and-down discords. Vanilla ice cream and ladyfingers followed.

About this time came my first ride in an automobile, an excitement which no child of today can recall. Before the modern infant's eyes can even focus he is slung in a hammock in the back of the family car; he gets his first conscious sight of the world wedged up between his parents on the front seat; and he can hardly talk before he is waving his father impatiently forward at green lights and squeaking warnings at red ones. At the turn of the century there were only ten or fifteen thousand automobiles in the whole United States, and although probably most of them were in and around New York people still stopped in the street to stare when one passed. A stare was all I knew about them until one day about 1900 my brother Maitland came down to Tenth Street to take my mother out in his new car. She disliked anything conspicuous, but had finally agreed to go for a short drive and to my intense excitement said I might go too. The law at that time forbade a speed of over ten miles an hour in New York City. This was liberal compared to the Red Flag Act, the first rule of the road in England, which fixed the speed of any automotive vehicle at four miles an hour and required that it be preceded by a man on foot carrying a red flag or at night a red lantern. But it was not liberal enough for Maitland.

His car was French, a Panhard, I think, open of course, with the door at the back. My mother had bound a scarf around one of her largest hats in preparation for the gales which were to be encountered, and I pulled my cap down to my ears. Maitland had on a Norfolk jacket, golf trousers and stockings, and goggles. My mother and I took our places bolt upright, facing each other, on padded seats like those in a buckboard. After one or two efforts, Maitland got the car started, moved it sedately along Tenth Street and then, picking up speed, turned into Fifth Avenue. For several blocks I watched a policeman on a bicycle pedalling along behind us and noted with satisfaction what a hard time he had keeping up; for it was difficult not to stall a car at ten miles an hour, and Maitland was probably doing twelve or thirteen. Eventually the cop overtook us and as was the habit in those days conveyed us directly to the station house in West Thirtieth Street. While Maitland went in to pay his fine my mother and I waited in the car outside, surrounded by little boys who called out derisively "P—e—e—nched! P—e—e—nched!" while making the appropriate gestures (and others) with their fingers. My mother sat there for what must have seemed an eternity, alternately pink and white with horror; and she did not get into an automobile again for several years.

Ranking with the first ride in an automobile for a child who has known only horses is a child's first sight, sound, smell and feel of the sea. That moment came for me at the age of five when Helen took me to spend a week at Seabright with family friends, the Shippens. The breakers were awesome, indeed terrifying. Sofie Shippen acknowledged to me later that she and her sisters, all experienced swimmers, had been rather callous about pushing nephews, nieces and other visiting children into the surf, to say nothing of misleading older friends who didn't know the treacherous Jersey coast. Once, she said, she had swum far out with "Dick" Davis—Richard Harding Davis—a powerful, well-built man, the most adventurous and renowned war correspondent of that day. She was foolish or perhaps mean enough to lead the way as far out as the fishpound; it was very rough, and he just made it. After they had rested a bit, holding onto the buoys, there was nothing for it but to start back for shore. This time she stayed behind, watched him disappear in the breakers, reappear, disappear again, and after a long time reappear again, then crawl up on the sand and lie there gasping. Sofie did not tease him about it; for one thing, she had been really frightened. Nor did she mention the incident to anyone. But he supposed that of course she would make a good story out of it, so he concocted one himself to the effect that he had asked her to marry him and she had replied by sitting on his head and

∾ 56

almost drowning him. So much for the report of a famous correspondent.

The Shippens had two Irish setters, Shamrock, sedate, with a noble head, and Annette, lithe, with an air of delicacy and intelligence. My father had spoken of the favorite hunting dogs of his youth, and many dogs had been part of the family at Danskammer, but these were the first dogs I myself became close friends with. In my mind's eye I see one of those little scenes that remain curiously clear after so much of importance has been forgotten. We sit at breakfast on the veranda the first hot morning. Shamrock and Annette are lying in the shade at a proper distance from the table. Sofie, in a shirtwaist with puffed sleeves, is teaching me a new and important skill, how to help yourself to honey neatly by twisting the spoon. The spoon is long handled, the honey jar deep, Sofie's hand brown and steady, mine clumsy; but I am just able (like Dick Davis) to make it.

Helen and Sofie had known each other since they were four—a friendship, in the end, of seventy-five years. But my sister Margaret set what must have been a more unusual record. As a baby she had been put on the lap of the Shippens' great-grandmother, old Mrs. Denning, of Fishkill, who lived to be nearly a hundred (she had given a glass of water to André on his way to execution); and not long before Margaret died she took a Shippen great-grandchild onto her lap, establishing thereby a physical touch between seven generations.

Somewhere about this time my weekly allowance went up from five to ten cents, with a pause for one year at, I think, seven. This was to take care of my ordinary expenses, such as the purchase of bull's-eyes or horehound drops out of a jar at Bigelow's drugstore on Sixth Avenue (still there—the store, not the jar) and black licorice gumdrops from a pushcart man (till these were forbidden, because he probably kept the trays under his bed at night). Enough had to be saved out to pay for materials to make presents or valentines; but Christmas was partly financed by an outright donation from Papa. Lent was a slim period; candy was out for the season, but there was always the mite box to be fed so that it would make a respectable thud when put in the plate at Sunday school on Easter morning. Extra pennies could be made by saving bottles for the junk man, who signalled his approach by the jingling bells strung on his pushcart and his cry, "Any bones, any rags, any bottles?" And there was always a quarter in the toe of the Christmas stocking.

For a time I entertained hopes of winning a prize by completing a set of the cards that came in certain grocery packages. When I started early breakfast, with only the waitress for company, the Postum in the china jug was not an invigorating prospect, and neither was the oatmeal that went with it, gluey, and with a somewhat thickened top from having waited too long. But oatmeal had one redeeming feature: it came with a card in each package—flags, ships, presidents, I forget what— and a full set entitled you to a handsome prize of large if unspecified value. As certain cards were persistently missing, I imagined that the manufacturer arranged his distribution so as to achieve this result. I determined to outwit him, and persuaded my mother to let me roller-skate around and buy each new box at a different store in some distant neighborhood; but with no luck.

In all proper households a special sense of excitement attaches to Christmas Eve, and in ours so much activity was concentrated in a few hours then that you felt confusedly that the time to go to bed, with the stocking there by the fireplace, would never come, and yet that it came all too soon. So that the edge should not be taken off Christmas by beginning the celebration too soon the wreaths and the tree must not be bought in advance, but on Christmas Eve itself. At Danskammer the tree had been marked long before, but it was not cut and brought home (on a sled, if luckily there was snow) till that evening. In the city we did our best to make up for this missing expedition.

In Christmas week, all Sixth Avenue from Macy's at Fourteeth Street to Siegel-Cooper's at Eighteenth was lined solidly with little stalls lit by kerosene lamps. Most were trimmed with greens and all were piled with useless gifts like brass paperweights, miniature Statues of Liberty or huge glittering gems pinned to cards, while the wires above were hung with necklaces and handkerchiefs and rows of striped peppermint canes. The hawkers called out their last-minute bargains, the smell of scorched holly and roasting chestnuts hung deliciously on the frosty air, and even the most garish objects seemed desirable in the flickering light. All the sights having been seen, and perhaps a last extravagant present purchased, the tree was bought and carried home, Papa at the large end, I at the small. The wreaths were hung in the windows and one was put around the front-door knocker, covering all but the griffin's claw. When it was time to trim the tree, decorations that dated back to the old Danskammer would be unwrapped with exclamations of recognition and hung in prominent places. Three even now survive—fish (minus spun-glass tail), rose (now hung to conceal the hole on one side), and small Santa Claus (fur cap missing). Then my stocking —for I was now the only one of stocking age—was attached to the nail which had survived the past year unnoticed under the nursery mantel shelf, and though I intended to keep my gaze fixed on it till morning, I was almost at once asleep.

After dinner Papa read the *Christmas Carol* aloud to the rest of the family in front of the fire downstairs. Everyone knew (as I did later) precisely what was in Scrooge's lumber room and could hear in advance the potatoes knocking on the lid of Mrs. Cratchit's pot. Marion recommended that when Papa reached the place where the knocker changes into Marley's face you should visualize the griffin's tongue protruding from it; that would double the eeriness. Not one word has ever seemed stale to me and the lump rises in my throat impartially for Tiny Tim and for little Scrooge alone in his schoolroom. Since the eighties, the initials of those gathered around the fire have been pencilled in the margin. At the start they filled the whole side of a page. Year by year, name by name, the list shortened.

VI

The wind blows out of the gates of the day.
—YEATS, "The Land of Heart's Desire"

WHEN I REACHED NINE OR TEN I COULD DO PRETTY much as I wanted with my spare time—the time, that is, not actually spent at school. This was not because of any theory about child upbringing but because the older ones in the family had gotten their education by being offered it, not by being forced to swallow it, and what had worked with them would assumedly work again.

The result was that when I wasn't reading, eating, sleeping or studying (in about that order of importance) I lived as much as possible on roller skates. From the first, I had despised the wobbly rubber-tired bicycle skates affected by most of the young who frequented Washington Square; I thought them slow and sissy, and took violently to the noisier, more trustworthy and much speedier four-wheeler. Henceforth my hands smelt of oil and my black stockings always needed darning at the knees. Sidewalks were identified by their texture—

some corrugated or scored with wavy grooves that could trip you, some of rough concrete that buzzed the soles of your feet, others of smooth slate that allowed maximum speed. Where there was glass in the pavement to light office basements, janitors would rush out and shake their fists at me, but on skates I could make circles round them, and returned often to do so.

I had learnt the geography of polite neighborhoods long ago, when my mother would take me along in the carriage which in winter she had once a week to pay calls on her friends—Washington Square, Gramercy Park, Stuyvesant Square (almost every house there full of relatives), up to Murray Hill and as far as the forties and fifties. The custom of New Year's calls was dying out, although a few old-fashioned gentlemen still held to it and appeared at the houses of their relatives and close friends to drink a cup of the hot milk punch that tradition demanded should be ready that day from eleven o'clock on. They left their overcoats and sticks in the front hall, but brought their silk hats into the parlor, placing their gloves in them before they laid them on a table, presumably to signify that this was to be a short appearance and not a real visit. Each gentleman wished to make as full a round as possible, and I have been told that by acting with great dispatch though proper ceremony he could pack in as many as fifteen. calls. Though this custom was vanishing, there still existed the institution of the "day," when the ladies of a certain neighborhood were expected to be at home.

In the Washington Square neighborhood the "day" was Friday, and I was stationed in the front hall to lead in visitors by the hand. At the age of three or four I took this duty seriously. There would be tea and hot chocolate in the dining room, as well as bouillon in a silver urn, also glazed importés and other little cakes from Dean's and such very small, very thin watercress sandwiches that they hardly seemed worth the trouble of eating. When my mother went to return calls on other "days" and took me with her I would sit conversing with the Irish coachman while she went inside briefly, for here too the idea was to get in a considerable number of calls.

I got to know the shopping districts too. Nearby on Broadway were Wanamaker's and Daniel's (Sons and Sons, why not grandsons?), Fleischmann's and Dean's; on Union Square were Brentano's and Tiffany's; and a bit further up on Broadway were the department stores and Purcell's and Huyler's (on a cold day there might be hot chocolate, but not if it was Lent). Fleischmann's bakery, next to Grace Church, was the place to stop at the right seasons for hot cross buns, election cake, Christmas cinnamon stars and New Year's cookies with caraway seeds, and at any season for little square sponge cakes; not for rolls—these were delivered fresh before breakfast, advancing civilization not having as yet required that they be picked up in a supermarket, limp in their cellophane. Bread was baked at home every other day and tasted like it. Fleischmann's bakery and sidewalk café were very animated in the daytime, but by nightfall a shabby queue stretched around the corner, where at the close of business the day's unsold bakings were distributed to the hungry. Brooks was on Broadway near Twenty-second Street, having by that date covered half of its northward migration from the corner of Catherine and Cherry streets. When my father was my age he had been taken to the old store far downtown for his first New York suit. Seventy years later he was able to describe it in detail: "The trousers were light grey, with a stripe down the side of dark grey, the jacket a blue roundabout with brass navy buttons." With it went red-topped boots into which he stuffed his trousers. When I was ten Brooks would have been surprised if my mother had brought me in for a blue roundabout. As it was, she took me to Best's or Stern's, and because such visits entailed trying on things I did my best to divert her into doing errands at other stores where I could wait outside, sitting on the steps and looking at life.

Now that I had my skates I was able to explore much further afield, at first the maze of small streets in Greenwich Village (this was before the Village swallowed up Washington Square), but soon ranging from Washington Market north along the waterfront to where the Atlantic liners came in. On Saturday mornings when a ship was about to sail I would hide my skates on the dock and go aboard. I got to know them all, the *Lorraine* and the *Savoie,* the old four-stack *Mauretania* and her competitor the *Deutschland,* the *Carmania* and the *Celtic.* The *Kaiser Wilhelm der Grosse* first came into port in the spring of 1906 and immediately became known as the "Rolling Willie." (As I walked nonchalantly up her gangplank, pretending I had come to see off a real departing friend, I had no idea of course that I would make a winter crossing in her as the transport *Agamemnon,* rolling just as nastily under her wartime name.) Each ship had its own ornate decor, its own band playing the right national tunes and its pleasant or cross library steward who would or would not give me the ship's postcards. Only the smell was generic—part grease, part linoleum, part fresh paint, part stale coffee, part leather and nicotine exhaled from the smoking room. I identified it then with the romance of the sea and only later learnt the mistake. Once romance came photographically near. Mary Garden summoned me to her side as a supernumerary in a going-away scene on the top deck—"a young admirer," the newspapers said the next day. She had just created the part of Mélisande, and everyone was talking about whether her voice was up to her looks; her looks, it was agreed, were stunning. Clasping me to her side, she assured me she was going to play games with me all across the Atlantic. I grinned inwardly even more than I did for the photographers.

My trips to Sunday school were hazardous, as bands of Micks used to lie in wait in the long crosstown blocks for the figure of fun I made in an Eton suit on roller skates. How better could they have used their time after Mass on a Sunday morning than in trying to keep a dirty little Protestant away from his heathen church? By varying my route, but thanks even more to my speed, I was able to arrive intact and without using the hockey stick I carried "just in case." I rather liked Sunday school, partly because getting there was a game, but more because my teachers were two soft and warm-hearted young girls, Dorothea and Ruth Draper. Ruth treasured my rendering of the First Commandment: "I am the Lord thy God. You'll never have another like me."

In Grace Church the Draper family sat directly in front of us; ranged according to age, they filled their pew even more snugly than we did ours. Ruth already used, without guile but not without effect, the lambent eyes which would so perturb later audiences. When Noel was home for the holidays her head would turn by imperceptible degrees until she could just glimpse him out of the corner of one eye. She would retrieve herself with a jerk, but in a moment, involuntarily, the head would begin turning again. His reply was to crack his knuckles nervously, something at which he was adept and which I greatly envied.

For me the scene was invested with special interest. The Dotty Dimple books, left over in my nursery from an earlier generation, recounted the adventures of a heroine named Flyaway. In Trinity Church a terrible mishap befell Flyaway; watching a friend across the aisle, she toppled over, bumped her nose and was hurried out in bloody confusion. Might Miss Draper just possibly lose her balance and suffer a similar fate? Such a diversion from Dr. Huntington's sermon was almost too awful to contemplate, but not quite. By the time I had turned the idea over in my mind thoroughly Dr. Huntington had finished.

The bountiful lady opening the bazaar, the immigrant girl in a shawl (Sargent's choice), the gymnastics instructress ("Got your lily, got your lamb?")—each picture of Ruth is unforgettable, but most clearly I see her in her little fur toque in the pew in front. She literally made the world her stage, but of all places I think she loved New York best. The last evening of her life, after finishing her performance at the theater, she told the chauffeur: "Drive me all over the city so I can look at the lovely Christmas lights."

In Lent, besides Sunday school and the usual church on Sunday morning there were services on Wednesday and Friday afternoons. The long aisles were dim, the hymns mournful, Dr. Huntington's sermons short but sombre. The main residue of all this church-going is not, I fear, what my mother intended, but nevertheless valuable—the respect for noble language that nobody can entirely fail to acquire, even if subconsciously, from hearing the King James Bible read week after week, year after year.

For some reason, I was taken to Dr. Huntington's funeral, and was much impressed by the long procession of bishops that marched two-and-two up the aisle—all except Bishop McVickar, several inches over six feet tall and so huge in every other direction too that he had to march one-and-one, and even so his vestments brushed our pew door as he passed. "Willy" McVickar, an intimate family friend, was Bishop of Rhode Island. His introduction to some members of his flock when he first arrived in Providence had been unconventional. He knew few people there, but with one family he was intimate; he had christened the children and had all sorts of little jokes with them. Still a newcomer in Providence, he walked around after church one Sunday morning to pay them a call. He rang the bell, was let in by the maid and went into the front drawing room. A hum of conversation came through the drawn curtains from the room beyond. Getting down on his hands and knees, he parted the curtains with his head and roared "Wouf, wouf!" When he looked up it was into the startled faces of complete strangers; the right street but the wrong house.

When I was nine the time came for me to go to a "real" school uptown, and unless it was pouring rain or snowing I went, of course, on skates. When the weather ruled this out I used the Fifth Avenue stage or the Sixth Avenue El.

On the stage I rode by choice on the outside, either perched up behind the driver or, if I was lucky, alongside him. You mounted to this vantage point by the hub and two widely spaced iron footholds. Thence, as the stage rumbled heavily along, New York unrolled before you. First came the sedate brownstone houses of lower Fifth Avenue; then the Flatiron Building, to some a thing of soaring beauty, to others an architectural monstrosity, but in everyone's eyes, including those on the top of the stage, a continuing wonder (height, 307 feet); then Madison Square with the Farragut of Saint-Gaudens, one of his best, conspicuous for all the passing traffic to see (until relegated by Mr. Moses to obscurity among the trees in the middle of the park); and the Worth Monument opposite, marking the burial place of the Mexican War hero, since invaded by a marble comfort station which hopefully does not disturb the general's bones. Then came the Holland House and the Brunswick Hotel, where in spring there might be a four-in-hand coach drawn up, making ready to tool up to Claremont or Pelham or out to Tuxedo, grooms holding the horses, while on top several feather-bedecked ladies preened themselves before a group of dazzled onlookers. On you went past the Waldorf up Murray Hill and along the old reservoir resembling an Egyptian tomb, afterwards replaced by the Public Library guarded by the two lions with Horace Greeley faces.

If you secured the seat beside the driver you took care not to interfere with a leather strap attached to his leg, for it performed an important function. Passing through an aperture under the seat, it led along the ceiling of the stage to the top of the rear door; and by it the driver controlled the door's opening and closing. When he stopped to take on passengers he moved his leg back, allowing the door to swing open by its own weight; then he would slide his leg forward, banging the door to, and start his horses off again. If you had to ride inside, where in winter it was stuffy and smelt of the stable, with a touch of kerosene added after dusk from the flickering lamp, the procedure was to wriggle your way forward and deposit your nickel in a box situated under the driver's seat. He could peer down through a small window and verify that your fare had been paid; if you were slow about it, he would mortify you by angrily thumping. If you needed change, you attracted his attention by ringing a bell and passing your money up to him through a small sliding panel; and he would hand the change back to you in an envelope colored according to the amount involved. Often there was much bowing by gentlemen offering to pass along the money for ladies, and sometimes an argument, in which everyone joined, as to whether or not a certain fare had been paid. When you wanted to get off you gave notice via the driver's leg by jerking the strap on the ceiling.

His various duties kept the driver busy, especially in winter when an extra horse was needed to help scale the slippery slope of Murray Hill. Gradually I became intimate with certain drivers, who let me help with

69 ❧

handing down envelopes; and when the stage was full I would wave grandly to groups waiting on the corners to signify that we couldn't stop.

My station for the Sixth Avenue El was at Eighth Street. When I reached the corner of Tenth Street and saw a train just rounding the curve from Bleecker Street I knew exactly whether or not it was worth while sprinting the two blocks and tearing up the long iron stairs to try to make it. If only the first car was in view I could catch it quite surely; if two or three cars, it would be a close shave; more than that, hopeless, and I could save my breath and leave my oatmeal and Postum untroubled in my innards. Sometimes, against all rules, the friendly ticket chopper would let me save a vital second or two by pushing my nickel into his hands rather than stopping for a ticked at the little wicket.

The El stations have been described as "Renaissance-Gothic in style, like a Swiss chalet on stilts." In winter, the atmosphere in the tightly sealed waiting room was semi-solid; the pot-bellied stove, with a mushroom top to spread the heat, mingled its coal fumes with the smell of tobacco juice from the spittoons and the powerful antiseptic from the "retiring rooms." When spring came, the colored-glass windows of the stations were reluctantly opened up, and on the trains you rode breezily on the car platforms, although there you missed the latest jingles of Phoebe Snow, the pleadings of the Gold Dust twins to let them do your work, Sapolio's report on the doings of the mayor, the butcher and other happy workers in Spotless Town, and the threats of the balding-headed man, "Going!—Going!!—Gone!! Too late for Herpicide!!!"

The beginning of school uptown coincided with my introduction to the dance, if attendance at Miss Benjamin's class can properly be said to have had much to do with dancing. Miss Benjamin, short and agile, wore a tight black bodice and a black silk pleated skirt, brief for those days, which made the black stockinged legs very prominent. Miss Winchester, younger, plump, in ruffles, was "at the piano," as they say in concert announcements. The pupils were ranged in two rows facing each other, boys on one side, girls (more of them) on the other.

"Never the twain shall meet" was the rule all winter. At Miss Benjamin's signal, Miss Winchester struck a reverberating chord, and simultaneously Miss Benjamin called out, "Advance right foot." A paused ensued, until the slowest-witted girl and the most reluctant boy had managed to do as directed. Miss Benjamin nodded, Miss Winchester struck another chord and Miss Benjamin called, "Bring up left foot." Then the directions were repeated, beginning with the left foot, and with explanations about turning step-by-step sideways, until each had come stiffly back to his or her original position. Nobody had the slightest inkling, of course, what it might feel like to do all this in rhythm and with a partner of the opposite sex.

My closest friend in the neighborhood, Giraud de Rham, was condemned also to go to Miss Benjamin's. To give each other encouragement, we went together; this had the added advantage that we could then be late and each alternately blame the other for having been delayed at home in starting. One afternoon when we arrived we heard Miss Benjamin already at work inside.

There in the hall stood a row of fur bootees, lined neatly up by the little girls' nannies; and there, conveniently near, stood a water cooler. Unhesitatingly Giraud put a glassful of water in each bootee. For some reason the crime was not traced to him, and as he did not have quite the nerve to confess, his scheme to be expelled from the class came to nothing.

In the spring the twain met. The event was looked forward to with dread, and properly. Each was assigned a partner, and doubtless the young lady found the strange boy who now advanced to meet her as repulsive as he found her. You were instructed to hold your partner at arm's length; this meant, if by good luck she wore a sash, that you grasped it to steady yourself and also in order to keep her from gradually drifting away into space. Rhythm was present only in theory, since Miss Winchester was continually being halted by Miss Benjamin in order to give time for someone to bring up that other foot. In those intervals the rest of the class held their pose, as though they were playing "Still pond, no more moving." Needless to say, I did not master the dance at Miss Benjamin's; nor did I until, much later, one of Marion's kind friends took me out by main force onto the floor of the Canoe Club at North Hatley and danced me around and around until I stopped counting, indeed stopped thinking at all about my feet, and simply waltzed.

The de Rhams lived in a "swell-front" house on the corner of Fifth Avenue and Ninth Street, built, I believe, by the Brevoort family. Outside, it was painted mouse color; inside, the spacious rooms and halls were mostly a greenish café-au-lait or chocolate. These rather depressing hues could not diminish the establishment's vast merits in my eyes. Not only did it possess a large garden on Fifth Avenue, with lilacs, roses of Sharon and forsythia; in the rear, opening onto Ninth Street, was a stable, not a disused stable turned into a studio as has happened now to the remaining stables in the neighborhood, but a stable with a pair of smart horses in it, a victoria for good weather, a coupé for use in winter, an Irish coachman full of anecdotes and amiability, and, above, a large loft with hay and straw, excellent for roughhousing and games. In the spring when we were not roller-skating together we played in the yard; in the winter we played in the stable loft.

Giraud died at St. Mark's the year before it became time for me to go to boarding school also. I sat through the funeral at Grace Church, the first funeral of a friend, in a daze of misery. No explanation was possible as to how it could be be that someone so manly and buoyant was snatched away, and I left.

During two winters, on two afternoons a week, I went up on my skates to the Seventh Regiment Armory, there to drill in the wavering lines of the Knickerbocker Greys with other unfortunates of assorted sizes. Two miles up in the morning to the Allen-Stevenson School, then on Forty-ninth Street, and two back; three miles up to the Armory, and three back; that made ten miles. But the skating part I loved and it never seemed long. I couldn't say as much for the drills. I suppose my parents thought it might be good for me to experience a sort of discipline I did not have at home; perhaps there was no more to it than the fact that one of the Shippen nephews had outgrown his uniform and I was able to inherit it. If it was the discipline, I resisted it; if it was the uniform, I in turn outgrew it. The trips in uniform were painfully conspicuous. However, this military interlude was so short that I never reached officer's status (which seemed to come automatically if one held on long enough) and thus mercifully was spared the encumbrance of a sword, which would have been much less useful in opening a way through unfriendly onlookers than my usual hockey stick.

A ritual of my daily skatings to school was to keep an exact record of the elapsed time of each trip. This I did in a small blue book which was always in my jacket pocket. It would have been no more fun to cheat about even a matter of seconds than it would be to cheat oneself at solitaire. The notebook is lost, but my recollection is that the best trips varied between fourteen and fifteen minutes. I was always trying, of course, to better my record. In those days very few traffic policemen were needed on Fifth Avenue, but there were two that played a big part in my life. One—tall, thin, dark, reserved—was stationed at Twenty-third Street, the other—robust, rosy-cheeked, smiling—a block higher up, where the Avenue crosses Broadway. They understood the importance of the record I was trying to set, and when they heard the toot of the whistle which I carried on a string around my neck they would hold up traffic so as not to delay me an unnecessary second.

I loved those two policemen, really loved them, especially my friend at Twenty-fourth Street. I made presents for him for Christmas at the same time I was making presents for my father, perhaps a packet of tissue paper to use in shaving, cut with nail scissors into a fat heart, held between highly ornamented cardboard covers, with a ribbon to hang it up with; or perhaps a pincushion made out of the toe of a red sock, stuffed with sawdust (procured from the butcher in Jefferson Market), sewn across the top by one of my sisters, and likewise suspended from a ribbon. On February 14 I would pause on my dash uptown to give him a home-made valentine, profusely decorated with pasted-on flowers and suitably inscribed. On St. Patrick's Day he got a knot of green ribbon, which he apologized for not being able to pin onto his uniform. Following my first trip abroad I went off to boarding school, so no longer saw him daily. However, it was a continuous preoccupation with me on that trip to find the right present to bring home to him, until in Venice I settled on a small picture frame in blue and pink mosaic. He always said he liked my presents, which he stuffed inside his helmet, and I never doubted my good taste.

In my goings and comings on skates I moved with agility; on foot, annoyed at being slow, I was forever bumping into something, barking my shins, raising a bump on my forehead, squashing a finger in a gate. It wasn't so much that I was awkward as that I was in a hurry. I have always liked to be here or there, not in between. The treatment for cuts was first soap and water, then water with carbolic. I was detached enough to recognize and appreciate the smell even while writhing under the sting. But I wasn't really strong and courageous, simply durable.

∾ VII ∾

Children are young, but not so young as people think.

—ENID BAGNOLD, "The Loved and Envied"

∾ TENTH STREET CHANGED SO LITTLE FROM YEAR TO year that I came to know something about every house on the block. I knew the feel of each bit of sidewalk so well that I could have skated to the corner of Fifth Avenue and, without raising my eyes, told which house I was passing, and then gone on to describe its inhabitants and the friendliness or reverse of the furnaceman, the butler and the cook. I knew everybody by sight, and experience had taught me which to speak to and which to avoid. One or two stately gentlemen disliked the whole tribe of rollerskaters so intensely that they stared stonily ahead as I whizzed past. Parents of my friends and friends of my parents usually gave me a wave.

John La Farge, who lived in the old Studio Building directly opposite, would have his eyes so fixed on his feet as he walked along, somewhat stooped forward, that though he often came to our house he noticed me no

76

more than any other passer-by. When he issued for a walk his Japanese valet followed a pace or two behind. But more often he would step into the cab which he always kept waiting so that if he had a sudden whim to go somewhere he would not be delayed even by the moment it would have taken the valet to fetch one from the corner. Such affluence was impressive.

"If Mr. La Farge is so rich," I asked, "why does he live in the Studio Building? There's no heat there and not much water."

I was told he probably liked luxuries such as the valet, the ever-available cab and good restaurants more than he disliked the lack of plumbing.

From time to time Mr. La Farge came over to borrow some object of art to use in his painting—a majolica jar, an ivory casket or a piece of Genoese velvet. These things would lie around in his studio until a day came when he was ill and imagined he might die, whereupon he would send the Japanese valet across the street with the whole accumulation. When he felt better he would begin borrowing again.

Mark Twain, who at one time lived in our block and later, I think, around the corner, was conspicuous because of his flowing mane and tie; but he looked rather fierce, and though I knew he stopped in to see my father occasionally, especially when he wanted advice about the decoration of his house in Connecticut, I don't remember ever daring to speak to him. If he noticed me skating by he gave no sign of it; he may have lost his liking for boys, but more probably was simply preoccupied with the business worries which were descending upon him.

In a row of several houses somewhat alike lived Mr. Godkin, the editor of the old *Evening Post;* Mr. Fowler, the Surrogate, top-hatted and elegant; the Mitchells, with several sons around Noel's age, who came in to box with him and were expert bicycle hockeyists; and an old gentleman with a foreign name and a goatee who sent out his butler to chase us away if we sat on his steps to tighten our skates. On the other side of the street was the double house of the Auerbachs, with a room large enough for an annual charity fair, always a disappointment because I invested heavily in the raffle and neither there nor anywhere else ever won anything.

As one progressed toward Fifth Avenue the houses became larger and the people living in them correspondingly more well-to-do. In one of these houses lived the prolific Ryan family. The children were exceedingly well brought up. On clear afternoons they were taken walking, in a graduated row of three, the largest on the inside, the smallest holding the hand of a governess on the outside. The square blue linen or serge collars of their sailor suits hung neatly over their blue reefers. The trio seemed to consist of the same children year after year. Actually, a new small one was added annually alongside the governess, while the largest was peeled off the other end and sent to boarding school. They looked with envy at Giraud and me as they broke ranks to let us skate through.

Next door to us, toward Sixth Avenue, lived my friend Timmy Coward. Mr. and Mrs. Coward I remember as rather vague about practical things, but hospitable and of interest because of their knowledge of the theatrical world. To make up for the Coward house having less depth than our twin houses did it had a proper yard where Timmy and I played with other boys of the neighborhood. This was the last of the nice houses toward Sixth Avenue, and all too soon it was pulled down to make way for one of the first apartment houses in the block. A loft building on the corner, opposite Jefferson Market Court, was occupied by a wholesale butcher. Great sides of beef, naked pigs and, worse, whole sheep with their heads still on, skinned but with eyes protruding, hung on trolleys in the doorway or were being trundled across the sidewalk into waiting vans. Until a new zoning law ended these activities one had to avoid skating on the greasy sidewalk.

At the opposite end of the block, on the corner of Fifth Avenue, lived old Mr. Eno, who was very rich indeed. He was considered a bit more than eccentric, even by my father who was an old friend. When he died a lawsuit developed over his will. Had he been *compos mentis?* One of the arguments used against him was that he could not even balance his checkbook. This struck so directly at my father that he reversed himself.

"Could not *even* balance his checkbook?" he asked with annoyance. "He was every bit as sane as I am!"

Few of our neighbors were about when I skated up to school early in the morning. Sidewalks were being brushed, doorways dusted with feather dusters, brass knobs polished. The milk and rolls had been delivered much earlier, but perhaps the Hygeia ice wagon was stopped outside a house while the driver sliced a cake of ice and prepared to carry it in with immense iron jaws; if the day was hot you secured a chip to suck as you skated along. Occasionally a gentleman might be taking a constitutional before breakfast. But the numerous early risers of the present day were missing; it was not considered kind to keep a dog in the city, except a lapdog.

Mr. Allen, one of the heads of the school uptown, was bald, formal and competent. Mr. Stevenson, the other head, was short, tweedy and colloquial. As I see Mr. Stevenson, who was almost too much of a good fellow, he is sitting on the edge of his desk with a pipe in his hand; I don't suppose for a minute he had a pipe in class, but the general impression he has left with me would make a pipe mandatory. He taught English, and tried to instill into his pupils his own genuine love of poetry. His method was to read aloud "The Lady of the Lake," which was bad enough, or "Sohrab and Rustum," which was worse; we would sit before him with glazed eyes, and then try to memorize the chunks which he assigned us. I can still reel off, without stopping to take the slightest thought, "The-stag-at-eve-had-drunk-his-fill-where-danced-the-moon-on-Monan's-rill-and-so-on-and-so-on-and-so-on." My liking for poetry, nourished by Miss Ruggles and more by my sister Helen, must have been strong to have survived.

School uptown was the signal for me to graduate to belted Norfolk jackets and knickerbockers that buttoned over the tops of woolen golf stockings. The improvement in looks—especially the disappearance of the dreary cotton stockings—was most satisfactory; I had begun to be conscious of appearances and like all other boys wanted to dress like all other boys. Maitland gave me a pair of gold cuff links for my birthday, indicating that he thought the time had come for me also to wear shirts with regular cuffs. With that came the threat of straight collars instead of round ones. I can see just how I stand in front of my mother's full-length mirror while my father from behind, hands over my shoulders, tries to help me knot the tie in one of the new collars (the name Belmont is seared into my consciousness). I saw the tie this way and that and jab the long collar button into my Adam's apple.

"I think I'd rather die right here," I exclaim, "than spend my life strangling in this thing!"

Actually, it was conceded that the old collars looked better for the present, and as things turned out I spent only a fraction of my life in starched servitude of any sort; for the war showed millions of Americans the comfort of soft collars and doomed anything else, just as the soldiers' Virginia cigarettes outmoded Melachrinos and Egyptian Deities.

On afternoons when I got back from school only in time to change and go uptown again to Miss Benjamin's or the Knickerbocker Greys I thought how much nicer it would have been to stay at home and read, especially if the weather made the streets unskatable. I hadn't learnt to read especially young even though helped by Marion, or perhaps because helped by her, for though she was conscientious she was impatient and this made me impatient to get to the end of the lesson too, by any means, even a row.

But when I was launched I read almost anything. The first children's books were inherited from my older brothers and sisters, whose favorite characters now came to life for me too: Beechnut, Malleville and Phonny of the Franconia stories, moving gently across the New

Hampshire summer or winter landscape; Mrs. Ewing's dashing Jackanapes; Mopsa the Fairy and the Water Babies; handsome Prince Giglio, boorish Prince Bulbo, detestable Princess Angelica and ragged Betsinda, repeatedly found to be really and truly Princess Rosalba; the visitors at Holiday House and the children in *The Tapestry Room* and Mrs. Molesworth's other stories. I laughed aloud over *The Peterkin Papers* as many times as I read them, which was often; the Lady from Philadelphia became a real person. I also inherited Howard Pyle's *Robin Hood* and *Pepper and Salt,* Hawthorne's *Wonder Book* (Walter Crane's as much as Hawthorne's in my eyes, for the pictures counted equally with the text), and *Swiss Family Robinson,* read and reread. There were dog-eared rows, too, of green *Harper's Round Table* and red *St. Nicholas,* besides a bound set of *Punch* going back to du Maurier and, further still, to Leech. I found out at once that there was nothing amusing or even understandable on the Charivari page, but the ladies with bustles and parasols and the gentlemen with tremendous mustaches or sideburns were funny even though what they said was not. Horatio Alger was absent, and for some reason I didn't care for Mark Twain until I read him again after I was grown up. *Tom Brown's School Days* I found depressing and I hated *Little Lord Fauntleroy. Peter Pan* was new and had become immensely popular, but not with me. Mowgli, the little frog, saved from Shere Khan at the mouth of the cave by Mother Wolf, shown to the Pack and passed by the Pack, was part of a scene that became only more real and more familiar and never less favorite as a result of renewed visits.

Mixed with this more or less natural fare were things less usual, picked at random because the titles took my fancy or because they happened to be within easy reach on a lower shelf. One such was a nice little set of *Tristram Shandy,* bound in tree calf, with Colonel Ward's bookplate in the front of each volume; likely they had helped him while away long evenings on his Revolutionary campaigns. It seemed to me tremendously comic, to be accounted for only by supposing that the complicated words (and the long *s*'s) made an intriguing sort of puzzle. Whatever the attraction, I perused the first volume far enough to decide that when I had a dog I would name him "Trim."

I also read and reread the *Morte d'Arthur,* including the parts skipped by Helen when she read it aloud. Parents need not worry that plain-spoken books will pollute their little darlings' minds; the young will understand them in the terms suitable to their age. When my daughter was about ten, Bobby Sherwood took her and his daughter to a matinee of *The Petrified Forest.* I asked her how she had liked it.

"Oh, it was wonderful," she said, "so funny. There was a scene outside a gas station. And the lady said, 'Let's have a tumble in the hay. I haven't had one for weeks!' Everybody laughed, for you see it was in the desert and there wasn't any grass."

Some of the things I tried were too long or too boring. I opened *Clarissa* and put it right back. The rows of Prescott and Parkman did not tempt me either (though before long Cooper did). Paul du Chaillu carried me easily through his adventures among the pygmies, helped by many woodcuts. I also came upon George Borrow and

83

became familiar with Romany life on the heath. Though I had a special feeling for the River I was not attracted by Washington Irving; I had a dislike for gnomes. I preferred *Kidnapped* to *Treasure Island,* though as I grew older I read both over and over. Eventually I went thoroughly through all Frank Stockton's adventures, also *Saracinesca* and other novels by Marion Crawford, urged by my father who always favored anything Italian. But when he tried me on the works of his friend Howells I put them aside and did not return to them until I was really grown up. For sentimental reasons he also recommended *Scottish Chiefs,* and here I was able to follow him. I took a particular liking for *How the Other Half Lives,* by Jacob Riis, and read it more than once, not out of any budding social conscience but because the stories and pictures were of people and things within my skating range.

The G. A. Henty stage was inevitable, and not a bad thing at all, for I learnt more history from *The Lion of St. Mark, With Clive in India* and dozens of others purchased at Macy's for nineteen cents than I ever absorbed at school. To get me away from Henty, Helen offered me twenty-five cents for each Dickens or Scott novel that I would read. Dickens I did not take to, except the un-Dickensian *Tale of Two Cities,* but I did better with Scott. Wisely Helen suggested *Quentin Durward* as a starter, the only one where the story begins on the very first page. Thence, not from avarice but because I gradually fell in with Scott's slow pace, I went through the whole list, even to the extremity of *The Black Dwarf* and *Anne of Geierstein.*

The red-bound set of *St. Nicholas* which went back to

its start in the seventies was kept up to date. Its regular characters became familiar friends, from Ralph Henry Barbour's Tom, Dick and Harriet to the Brownies. When I wrote Palmer Cox and told him of my feeling for the Brownies he drew me one of my own. As time went on, impelled more by a competitive than a creative urge, I took part in the activities of the St. Nicholas League, a nursery for many real talents such as those of Elinor Wylie, Bobby Sherwood and Steve Benét. I solved puzzles and sent in puzzles to be solved; I took snapshots, wrote stories and even tried verse. I achieved a silver medal, then a gold one and eventually (for puzzles, probably, rather than anything literary) the supreme glory of the Cash Prize, one dollar.

I recovered my liking for poetry after Mr. Stevenson ceased to work at it, despite the fact that occasionally my father would punish me by assigning a verse to be copied out neatly a specified number of times. Once in North Hatley he set me the first verse of "Elegy Written in a Country Churchyard." I had heard somewhere that the words in the third line could be rearranged in a great number of combinations, each making sense; so this I did in as many versions as I could devise. When I handed in my paper my father must have been amused but he was careful not to show it, and I had to sit down and do my stint over again while my friends who were waiting outside in the garden to go swimming waited still longer because I had been a show-off.

When I was really small and ill or restless at bedtime, Helen used to take turns with my mother sitting with me, and she would always be willing to say over, as many times as I wanted, some of the poetry she liked best. It might be sad, but I never minded; her hands were cool, her voice calm. She would say "Divided," by Jean Ingelow (one of the saddest, after a gay beginning), Clough's "Say not the struggle naught availeth" (which I liked the sound of, though the sun through eastern and western windows was confusing), and Rossetti's difficult

> 'Who owns these lands?' the Pilgrim said.
> 'Stranger, Queen Blanchelys.'
> 'And who has thus harried them?' he said.
> 'It was Duke Luke did this:
> God's ban be his!'

I particularly liked Longfellow's verses about Portland harbor, a favorite with my father too, and the part in the *Idylls of the King* where Elaine in her tower to the east is guarding the sacred shield of Launcelot. Each time Young Lochinvar whisked away his bride from under the noses of her haughty kinsmen it gave me fresh satisfaction. Helen preferred Christina Rossetti and Emily Dickinson, and was apt to include "Does the road wind uphill all the way?" and "I never saw a moor." I was uncertain that I understood either, but I felt them in the pit of my stomach, which Housman says is the true center of poetic feeling. When I was older I became familiar with Helen's three little volumes by Emily Dickinson bound in pale green, white and gold, and well worn long before she acquired fame. In time Helen would usually come to Owen Meredith's verses beginning, "At Paris it was, at the Opera there," and if she didn't I would ask for it. I felt the spell of the jasmine flower even though I had never seen or smelt one, and I waited for the tenor's "Non ti scordar di me." I had no idea what it meant but agreed with the poet that it must be soothing even to souls in purgatory. (Long afterwards I chanced upon a revised edition of Meredith and found that this best-remembered line had been edited out.) As a matter of course there were "Kubla Khan" and "The Lady of Shallot," besides much more, most of it forgotten by the mind but none of it really lost.

Never really lost. Just as the silver doorknob to which my mitten froze as I waited outside the house on Washington Square will always be colder than anything Amundsen found at the South Pole, so the sound of the mirror as it cracked from side to side comes back unexpectedly like the sharp report of the ice breaking up in the River, and the caverns measureless to man remain deeper for me than any abyss in the ocean bed.

VIII

In a land of clear colors and stories,
In a region of shadowless hours,
Where earth has a garment of glories
And a murmur of musical flowers.

— SWINBURNE, "Dedication"

WHEN THE MAGNOLIA FLOWERS OPENED IN THE Beekmans' front yard I began counting first the weeks and then the days till we would board the train for Canada. When finally the Day arrived we had lunch at the Saint Denny, a sedate old house on Broadway nearly opposite Grace Church. The elderly colored waiters, who knew Papa well, bustled to serve him. As we squeezed into the Pullman car through the narrow passageway, trying desperately to hide the canary cage under its pillow slip, everything was as it should be. The steam pipes, still warm from the previous day's run from the north, gave full value to the exhausted atmosphere's familiar aroma of dried-out plush, cinders and varnish. The same jolly porter put out extra pillows in the stateroom and went through the motions, knowing the effort was vain, of opening one of the windows. As my mother pointed out, there was a little screen outside, proof that the window was supposed to open; to which he remarked how fortunate it was that it wouldn't since if given a chance the cinders banked up inside the screen would bury us before morning "as deep as Pittsburgh."

This evidence that things remained as they always had been promised that the summer ahead would be unchanged from the past, than which nothing better could be imagined.

The journey would hardly be long enough for all the pleasures in view. There was a careful check to be maintained on whether we were running on time. There was the canary to be kept quiet so that the conductor would wink at the breach of regulations. There were games to be played with members of the family who took me on in turns to moderate my excitement. We "packed my grandmother's trunk," we "loved my love with an A" and all the other letters including "X," for which "Ex" was a permitted substitute, and inevitably we played "Statistics," in which you and your competitor count the animals on your respective sides of the train. The lowest score, one, was for a cow or a horse (what would a horse rate today?), while top value was for a black cat on a windowsill, a conceivable phenomenon on drives from Danskammer to Newburgh but highly unlikely along a railroad track; nevertheless it remained a hopeful possibility. Once some Barnum and Bailey cars on a siding at Bridgeport introduced a galaxy of unheard-of factors and ended the game in confusion.

At last Hartford would come. It was important because there the basket with cold chicken and graham bread sandwiches would be opened, along with the bottle of claret diluted with water, or rather water colored with claret, which Mamma considered hygienic on train trips. The change to the Boston and Maine at Springfield was usually made in a hurry. Once, however, when there was a delay, my inquisitive forefinger, reaching up onto the cigar counter, felt around until it found a small hole into which it just fitted, whereupon the tip was snipped off. The tiny scar is still there.

Nothing could be seen through the window with the screen; but long before there was even the promise of daylight I was stealthily peeking under the flap of the other window shade to see what progress we were making. At last the grey dawn began to reveal station names that were familiar—Ways Mills, Newport, Derby Plain. At "the Line" the customs man paused only long enough to say he was glad to see us again. At Ayers Flats (later elevated, with no act of God to warrant it, to Ayers Cliff), we were at the head of Lake Massawippi. The train swooped along the lake shore, bucking and jibing (even mixed metaphors are inadequate) for what seemed an eternity of apprehension (sometimes worse), in fact about thirty minutes, until we climbed down at North Hatley, green under our cinders.

The first summer, 1900, Papa had taken a cottage at North Hatley sight unseen. "Plum" Le Baron drove us over from the station in his buckboard, and as we drew near Papa's face fell. The cottage stood at the top of a steep bank, brown already in June, with upright sections of clay drain pipe ranged in front of the abrupt porch, each filled with earth and supporting a magenta petunia. At one side stood an immense iron "potash pot," used for rendering soap in settler days, now overflowing with chickweed and more petunias. Across the roof, in yellow letters a foot and a half high, was written DREAMLAND.

Papa always saw things as they could be rather than as they were, and I think it was almost a compulsion with him to buy the place that autumn so that by spring he could start bringing out its possibilities, hidden to all but him. The tiny windows which would open only five inches at the bottom were made into wide casements. The irregular floorboards in the sitting room, painted lead-color in an ineffectual effort to hide their roughness, were planed and waxed. The dentist's chair and the folding chairs with carpet or canvas tacked in loosely for seats (flapping eerily when the door opened) were replaced with chintz and wicker, while a local carpenter made additional furniture to Papa's specifications. What had been described as an "annex" was a barn, one side filled to the roof with slabs of ice buried in straw, the other deep in manure. Papa made half of it into a studio, half into a bedroom, and raised the roof to make another room and an attic.

The barnful of manure was just the thing needed for the brown bank and the lawn below, where Marion and her friends laid out a tennis court the following summer, and for the garden terraces which Papa began constructing from fieldstone, helped by a muscular humpback, Frank Beauregard. (For twenty-five years Frank called Papa "Mr. Hamstring.") The four relentlessly pyramidal sprucelings that stood in a row at the foot of the bank were not the red cedars of Danskammer or the cypresses of Rome, but they became a useful shield between the cottage and the road, and the little stream at one side where I caught crayfish and hair snakes was soon bordered with cardinal flowers and maidenhair. What with Papa's energetic gardening and more and more manure (Mr. Spriggins' bills read "Manure and me $8.00, Manure and Harthur $6.00"), the flower beds spread to every corner of the little place and the short Canadian summers brought masses of flowers all pell-mell together. For the shady spots, it was understood that when any of us went on expeditions we would bring back dolls' eyes, Solomon's-seal and other wood things, and of course more clumps of maidenhair.

The village was hardly more than a hamlet when we came, with a general-store-and-post-office near the bridge ("Walk or Pay $2") where the lake emptied into a tributary of the St. Francis. Our next-door neighbors, the ancient Miss Wadleighs, both of whom lived to about ninety, had come as girls to teach school at the settlement by the bridge. In the earliest days, they said, the French had called the place *L'Outlet,* but although farmer families averaging a dozen children or more kept the countryside solidly French, the village itself became English, and when this happened the more prosaic name was adopted. In the first years we took our meals at the Miss Wadleighs', notified by a dinner bell to come across through a little gate in the intervening screen of rosebushes, currants and gooseberries. There was no need to tell us the vegetables were "garden fresh": the bent forms of the old ladies were daily in the garden, hoe in hand, and when the new peas and lima beans came, and then corn by the dozen for both dinner and supper, we forgot the days of grey hash and turnips.

Back of the house a long hillside sloped up to groves of sugar maple, and beyond stretched what we knew as the Downs, where rocky outcroppings alternated with stretches of sweet grass, thyme, bracken and spirea, one of many favorite places for afternoon picnics. As we lay back in the bracken, the undulating Canadian forest stretched out before us, uninterrupted to the north and west as far as Mt. Orford except by the silver strip of Little Lake Magog and in the distance where a tiny thread of smoke revealed the passing of a Canadian Pacific train, headed in our lazy imagination for Manitoba and Saskatchewan. The blue mass of Orford, flat against the setting sun, merged gradually with the deeper tones of its own lengthening shadow.

The hillside was a pasture when we first came, but gradually it was spotted with groups of birch and poplar saplings, chokecherries and hazelnuts. Patches of raspberries and blackberries were everywhere, and in the fall there were wild plums and, with their unaccountable irregularity, mushrooms in such profusion one year that you couldn't collect them all, the next couple of years none at all. I gathered everything industriously. Old Miss Alice Wadleigh, however, looked up the hillside with the eyes of her frontier youth.

"I hate to see the forest creeping in," she said bitterly. "Those meadows cost our men a pretty bit of trouble."

When we looked south from the hilltop, over the maple groves and the shanties used for the sugaring-off in March, Lake Massawippi lay directly at our feet. (Margaret said maples are like middle-aged women who have lost their figures and don't care.) The left shore was lowish and uninteresting, as indicated by the name of its sole feature, Point No Point. The other side was what made the lake worth while. First came Black Point, sweeping up in wooded folds from a headland of mossy rock, cedars, white birch and springs in ferny dells. Two or three miles further on was Blue Point, slightly opalescent in the summer haze that gave it its name, but as clear-cut as Black Point in blowy autumn weather, when every branch on the topmost ridge, every twig almost, stood out distinctly against the blue Canadian sky and the piled-up clouds.

Between Black and Blue Points curved a wide bay, edged with pebbly beaches and two or three little camps. There, from the time my friends and I got to be ten or twelve, we spent as much of our time as possible. Before the first war it was not the custom for school and college boys to take summer jobs, which meant that there always were half a dozen boys about my age at Hatley; and where the boys were the girls were also. We grew up together in a happy crew that varied little from year to year, unconscious that later generations would not enjoy our freedom, for the boys would be learning to load and unload Coca-Cola trucks and to wait in summer hotels; and where the boys were not the girls would not be either. From then on Hatley declined.

Off Black Point the lake was so deep that the bottom could not be plumbed with the longest fishing line; at least so we told each other, though we never tested it. In these bottomless pools lake trout lurked; and once or twice a year somebody caught one to prove it. What were really abundant enough to promise an almost certain evening meal were black bass and perch, and sometimes if one trolled for lake trout one caught a pike.

We constantly canoed up the lake, often to spend a night at some little camp.

A favorite place was the Hermit's—the Hermit now a legend, but his cabin still there, set in a small clearing thick with raspberries and blackberries. The surrounding woods were silent except for the occasional angry call of a Canada jay or, at dusk particularly, the flutings of a hermit thrush. At the end of the long plank improvised into a dock the lazy perch looked sideways at you, undisturbed by the dartings to and fro of the nervous little shiners; water spiders skittled across the surface. Jewelweed hid the stream that came over mossy rocks from the spring up the ravine, bringing with it a whiff of balsam and wood fern. From across the lake the faint pad-pad of the evening train reminded us to get out of our bathing things and make the fire for supper.

If I describe how the girls dressed—middy blouses, wide pleated serge skirts, black stockings, hair tied with bows—they will sound like a basketball team from a reformatory. I can only say that to us they were beautiful. Even when we were camping the bathing costumes were more decorous than decorative. Boys wore flannel trunks and woolen tops (it is hard to recall that as late as the thirties a man would be arrested on any public beach near New York if he went swimming without a top). The girls were completely covered in black or navy blue from a neckline that would have been approved by Mrs. Calvin Coolidge, who once described the neckline of her evening gowns as "one hundred percent American." Frilly sleeves extended almost to the elbows. The bloomers were not visible, except by mischance, for the skirts covered them to below the knees. The bloomers joined long black cotton stockings. Unlike less emancipated creatures at Bailey's Beach in Newport, however, they did not wear black gloves or straw hats in the water. In spite of their impediments, they could swim, dive and paddle. They also could cook, and well. The evenings around a bonfire were easy and free and innocent. Each of us knew which girl he wanted to paddle home, but no exclusive proprietorship was expected or accorded.

If we were spending the night in camp we had to persuade some grownup to go along as chaperon; she was pampered and not allowed to cook or wash dishes. That was as far as we expected or needed to be looked after. Parents did not feel called upon to organize their children's "activities." We were more than able to amuse and take care of ourselves.

In the early days when North Hatley was still very small and the same families came back year after year, life centered almost exclusively around the lake; yet even then there were other diversions. The first excitement of the summer came with Dominion Day and, four days later, the Fourth of July. The village had enough patriotism to celebrate both national holidays exuberantly and without thought of rivalry. On Dominion Day morning there was a parade led by the mayor, Jean Le Baron, with flags and floats; sometimes, even, a pair of Mounties appeared. In the evening there was a concert by the village band. The summer people helped decorate the floats and joined in applauding the mighty efforts of the band, led by Frank Turcotte, who blew a stentorian trumpet, at the same time gesticulating with it wildly in the effort to keep his cohorts together. My Fourth began as early as my father permitted and lasted as long as my firecrackers. In the evening, the countryside flocked in from miles around for the fireworks. There were frantic cavortings and neighings from the horses hitched to the buggies along the lake front; at that date they had not been hardened even to an automobile, much less to a roman candle.

No word can be used to describe the North Hatley Band except terrific, either when it was divided in opinion as to whether it was playing "When Irish Eyes Are Smiling" or "Turkey in the Straw" or when all the members rose solemnly at the end and played, almost in unison, "God Save the King." Frank Turcotte furnished the music also for the weekly Canoe Club dance. But the Canoe Club was mainly what its name implies: it was a little shingle building with a landing float and a raft, also a piazza where those who were not paddling, sailing or swimming could watch those who were. I named my dinghy, and aptly, the *P.S.* I preferred a canoe. Captain Blue was in charge.

"Wait till I get a sponge," he'd say, "and dust out that water."

In the annual regatta we all competed in everything. Parents crowded the porch and the younger children lined the roof, their legs hanging down over the heads of their elders in a sunburnt fringe. Noel, whose arms were of iron, usually won the single paddle. His chief competitor, who won when Noel happened to be away, had a histrionic temperament; when Noel was there, and defeat loomed inevitable, he slumped fainting over the front thwart. The noisiest race was between "war canoes," girls and boys four strong in each, usually with gunnels awash before the finish. Two specialties were the crab race, in which you knelt in the extreme bow of the canoe, and the deck race, in which you crouched on the tiny "deck" in the rear. I became expert in the hurry-scurry, where agility counts more than strength. At the judge's pistol you jump free of your canoe, scramble back in, repeat the same a couple of minutes later, and if you are lucky finish with your canoe only half full of water.

The first "library" at Hatley consisted of two or three shelves of tattered volumes, antiquated even then, housed upstairs in Jean Le Baron's general store and for rent for five cents a week. Later Mamma and other ladies, both summer and resident, established a lending library which eventually, thanks to innumerable benefits, had a building of its own and over the years acquired a remarkably good collection of books. The library was open each morning, and the various ladies interested took charge in turn.

One noontime I met Mamma just as she reached our gate after "her day" at the library. She was turning to walk back because, she said, she had forgotten something.

"Let me go for you," I said.

"No, it's nothing anyone can do but me."

"Then wait till tomorrow," I insisted.

"No, I prefer to do it at once."

When she returned half an hour later, very warm, I asked what it had been that I couldn't do and that couldn't wait.

"I forgot," she said, "to enter the fines for the day and put the money in the cashbox."

"How much was it?" I asked.

She demurred, but finally, turning pink, admitted that it had been two cents.

"It is the principle of the thing," she said; "the money did not belong to me."

I was proud whenever Noel would take me anywhere, but never more so than one September when he said he would try to "give me a shot at a deer." I was eleven, and though I knew how to handle a .22 I had never used a larger caliber and had never aimed at a living target. We put our canoe onto a hay wagon and were driven over to Little Lake. The air had the "cold underneath" feeling of autumn in Quebec, but the sun was still warm when we pitched our tent on a bit of level ground where the Magog River comes into the lake. We trolled along the edge of the long grass, caught a pickerel, fried it for supper, watched some hell-divers upending near the flats, saw the moon rise, heard and then half-saw a dim V of geese moving southward on their appointed way, and snuggled into sleeping bags. Mine was misnamed, for I was much too keyed up to sleep.

When the stars grew pale I nudged Noel and he paddled us silently through gentle swirls of mist to what he thought was a likely spot for deer to come down to the water. A long wait followed, but no deer appeared among the tamarack and swamp maples. The small detail that I had not shot or even seen a deer could not diminish my satisfaction at having been on a "hunting trip."

I knew the first part of the road to Little Lake well. It forked at Minton (a crossroads with a white Univer-

salist church, nothing more), one fork going on down a
long, long inclined plain to the lake, the other branch-
ing off to the right through *habitant* farmland and
eventually solid forest; here the road became "cordu-
roy," and at the end was the hamlet of St. Elie. On fall
afternoons when I was still quite small Marion used to
take me on long walks. Usually the route led through
Minton, sometimes up a rocky road past the slag heap
of a forgotten copper mine, sometimes around what we
called "the big square." Once we had gotten as far as
St. Elie before Marion realized that the round trip
would be eight or nine miles. My legs almost crumbled
with weariness and we had to sing "Onward Christian
Soldiers" at the top of our voices to manage the last
mile home.

On a stony farm five or six miles beyond Minton lived
an Englishman, Mr. Pears (pronounced, he said,
"Peers"), with a large family, a grand manner and titled
relatives about whom he talked in imprecise terms but
often. His wife was vague and distracted, utterly lost in
a French-Canadian near-wilderness, hemmed in for six
or seven months of the year by snow, mud and washed-
out roads. The five children were all boys and all under
ten. Our doctor at North Hatley told my mother of going there one winter's evening to see after Mrs. Pears,
who had just escaped giving birth to a sixth child, and
finding the other five huddled in one bed for warmth,
no fire in the kitchen stove and hardly any food in the
house. The next spring my mother remembered to
bring up a trunkful of clothes that Noel and I had outgrown, and sent them over by the doctor along with
some extra blankets from our cottage. As an after-

thought she put in half a dozen books. In due time a formal note came to Papa from Mr. Pears, thanking him for the books; nothing else mentioned. Living with them for a time—it must have seemed to him a long, long time—was a handsome English boy of about eighteen who had been lured by Mr. Pears' advertisement in a London paper to come out to Canada to "learn agriculture." For the privilege of slaving on this derelict farm he had paid a premium and his ocean passage and was now paying monthly board. As part of his equipment for the new world he had brought evening clothes and a high hat in a leather hatbox. It was two years before he could find the money to escape.

The doctor had been a classmate of Sir William Osler's at McGill and felt himself capable of greater things than were afforded by the practice at North Hatley and in the outlying French-Canadian countryside. And indeed he was; he had a first-rate mind and real intuition, but he was continually frustrated by his isolation from the medical world and sometimes in boredom became slack. I can see him sitting by my bedside, taking up a bottle of cough medicine that had been brought from New York, shaking it and then licking the cork to see if he approved of the contents. Recollecting himself, he looked guiltily at my mother, then found a way out by saying, "No, that's stale, throw it away." He told Margaret that when the time came for him to deliver the twelfth child in a French-Canadian family he would caution the father that though twelve was a lucky number, thirteen was unlucky. The next year the thirteenth would come along just the same.

Another road passed below Minton, went around the

upper end of Lake Memphremagog and took you eventually to Mt. Orford. "Plum" Le Baron and his buckboard could be hired for a day's expedition there—a long day, for you started early, climbed the mountain (not mountaineering, but a tough climb through wind-bent trees and over tumbled boulders), cooked supper at the foot, and drove home by moonlight, too tired to talk. In late summer, the northern lights would often stream in glory up to the very zenith, sometimes cold pink, sometimes the pale green of the inside of a catnip leaf.

By 1910 the automobile was no longer totally unknown in these parts. When a streak of dust appeared in the distance everyone got out, and old Plum held the horses tightly by the bridle till the monster had passed. If the driver of the car was considerate he stopped by the side of the road so that the trembling horses could be led by. We thought these encounters rather fun, but when a *habitant*'s horse backed his buggy into a ditch he would shout French invectives at the motorist and threaten to shoot the next one that came along "his" road.

The glide of a canoe is the most soothing of all motions, and from the eddies of your paddle in smooth waters at night come, to my ears at least, the most seductive of all sounds. If you know how to handle a canoe it also responds to your instant needs in the passage down rough rivers.

Other boys and I often went on canoe trips, sometimes lasting several days, once on a long trip, carefully prepared, to fish for trout in the heavily lumbered swampland beyond Megantic. But the favorite expedition was a short one which we used to make down the

Massawippi River a couple of times each summer. The water ran smooth as far as the sawmill. But after you had carried around the dam and the cavernous banks of sweet-sour sawdust overhanging the current just below it, you entered a series of rapids, treacherous because shallow. On the map it was the same river each year, but for the voyager it was always new—a swift succession of white curls which showed submerged rocks, of up-ended stumps hazardously caught between boulders, and of smooth green gullies, the instantly chosen aisles through which a canoe could safely slip. Calm stretches intervened, and a covered bridge let through wisps of hay and patches of light where years of frost and sun had rotted the planking and even the old hand-hewn timbers. At Eustis, once a copper-mining village, now only a lonely church and two or three houses, you passed barren slag heaps, then came to a series of meadows almost as lovely as the banks of the River Wye, with great elms standing grandly by themselves and thickets of hazelnut and chokecherry dipping into the water. There followed another set of rapids, partly jammed with sunken logs rejected by the sawmill upstream, leaving only a channel so close under the bank that you had to duck your head to escape the low-hanging bushes. And then, rounding a last curve, you were within sight of the Lennoxville station, just in time to scramble up the cinder bank and shove your canoes aboard the two-car evening train back to North Hatley. The conductor was too friendly to charge for them.

"It's only ten miles," we'd say.

"It's just baggage," he'd agree.

And so home, soaked and tired, hungry too, for the

perch caught below Eustis had been cooked and eaten ages ago, along with the crackers and McLaren's cheese in its neat china jar, and the quarts and quarts of boiled coffee into which we had dropped an eggshell on the theory (was it an illusion?) that it settled the grounds.

On Sundays everyone went to the morning service at St. Barnabas, the Anglican church. A newcomer expressed surprise at the name: "I never knew Barabbas was a saint." It must have been a difficult charge for the clergyman, whose congregation overflowed the little shingled building in summer but dwindled to a handful in winter, and who also had a church to look after several miles away at Waterville and besides held services at the mission chapel at Eustis. The children were all in clean clothes and slid around uncomfortably on the varnished pew seats. Nevertheless, the first clergyman that I remember, Mr. Tams, held us in fascination. He stuttered badly, and we hung on each difficult word with more embarrassment than he did and when finally he brought it out like an explosion we sometimes gasped with audible relief. To make up for the slow delivery, he read the lessons with a roar.

"My father chastised you with *w-w-whips!* But *I*"—he would continue menacingly—"will chastise you with"—then a long struggle—"*scor—r—r—*pions!*"

He was a good man, very sincere, and lasted several years.

The choir, small and voiceless in winter, large and voiceless in summer, could not drown out the squeak of the organ pedals and the wheeze of the bellows. To make up, the young in the congregation shouted out "Ten thousand times ten thousand" and "Jerusalem the golden" with zest. We prayed for the King, the Queen, George, Prince of Wales, the Princess of Wales and all the Royal Family, and also by a courteous reciprocity for the President of the United States and all those in authority. On the whole we rather liked our summer church; it was small, light, airy and convivial compared to city churches, and afterwards we collected outside and planned what to do that afternoon.

The Harvest Home service came late in the autumn, after almost all of the summer people but us had left. Sheaves of corn with pumpkins at their feet stood on either side of the chancel, and red apples outlined the altar and were ranged on the windowsills. After one of these services on a cold grey Sunday I found the following scribbled by my sister Helen on the back of an envelope:

> The Rector preached and preached,
>   I thought he would never cease;
> He spoke of our beautiful Harvest Home,
>   Of the wonderful year's increase;
> He mentioned the fields we had tilled,
>   The curious nature of seed,
> He said how delightful that we should be filled
>   When most of the world was in need;
> He told of the sun in his strength,
>   Of the former and latter rain,
> And when he had said it at length
>   He said it over again.

There were several "characters" among the summer visitors. Old Mrs. Queen, during a dry spell, leaned over our fence and advised Papa to get a longer hose so he could put one end in the lake and water with the other. Genial Cap'n Tawm Pinckney loved to fraternize with Northerners, but his wife, retaining the bitterness of many Confederate women long after their menfolk had forgiven if not forgotten, did no more than bow to them in the street though she would go to their homes for a quiet hand of euchre. Mrs. Daves, a dignified old lady, was escorted from her blazing house carrying her "potty" which she had not had time to use beforehand. Mrs. Queen was, figuratively speaking, one of quite a hierarchy. A family named King came from Providence in the summer and another named Prince from Boston. Indigenous were the numerous Le Barons, while the "Eating Hall" where some summer folk took their meals was run by bulging and good-natured Mrs. Le Duc.

At the Canoe Club dances there was continuous cutting in; "going steady" had not yet settled boy-and-girl relations into solemn routine. The slow whine of the Boston alternated with vigorous one-steps. In the Boston Dip the girl stuck out a tense leg to the rear, went down till the knee almost touched the floor, but kept the upper part of her body rigidly erect facing her partner. There had to be at least one Virginia Reel in the course of the evening because Bill Murray, six feet two and skinny, who didn't dance, wanted to participate to the extent of blowing the whistle. One summer—it must have been 1914—I returned from a visit to Newport with the score of the first fox trot ever heard or danced to on these shores. Conrad, whose band was so unrivalled in New York in those days that you chose which dance to go to more by whether he was playing there than by whose party it was, had just gotten a fox-trot orchestration from Europe—something about "mein lieber süsser Bubi"—and made a simplified version of it for me to take back to Hatley. When Turcotte looked at it he said he thought someone had hoaxed me; and when he and his pianist and drummer rendered it for the first time my friends agreed. When they got home in the fall, however, they found that the one-step was in fact yielding its long-time supremacy, though as yet they did not know, of course, that the tide was now set via the fox trot for the jazz age.

Once a summer everybody was mobilized for the church fair. We made maple fudge and pulled molasses candy; pasted labels on jars of raspberry and blackberry jam of varying consistency from watery to solid rock; and cut balsam to make pillows. Our elders baked layer cakes and performed various feats of fancywork, and those who had Southern cooks contributed trays of beaten biscuit. In one bad period there was a vogue for burning wooden boxes and leather articles with red-hot needles, one of the smelliest of modern "arts and crafts." My efforts to discover the right sweet grass such as the itinerant Indians used to weave baskets was a failure. But one summer I acquired a jig saw and began cutting picture puzzles. As I avoided boring scenes of browns, greens and vast expanses of sky and cut the pieces into animals and other realistic shapes, the puzzles were such a success at the fair that I went into the business afterwards on my own account.

It usually happened, too, that someone turned up with such abundant energy that there was no escaping a benefit for the Library or the Village Improvement Society. It might be a vaudeville, composed of a Flora-dora sextette of brawny boys, a classical dance in which little girls in cheesecloth presented offerings to Ceres while a chorus sang the Song of Proserpine, and a row of minstrels who exchanged local quips and sang topical verses to "Everybody Works but Father," "Git Up, Napoleon, It Looks Like Rain," "So Long, Mary" or a tune from the new hit, *The Pink Lady*. In an embarassing scene I was one of the Gracchi, paired with an even younger friend; when Cornelia declaimed, "These are my jewels!" it was too much for the other jewel, who darted off into the wings amid applause from his relatives. One summer Mrs. Jarley exhibited her waxworks, another there was a Book Party, and another there was a life-size *Punch and Judy*, in which Margaret was a slinky and very animated Devil, menacingly flapping a long tail. When a make-believe stuffed devil was eventually flung over the footlights a shriek arose from the very young, who thought Margaret herself was being sacrificed.

There also was an annual baseball game between the boys and girls. The boys wore long skirts and had to bat left-handed, but even thus handicapped they won, for many of them were on college teams. Everyone sat around on the grass, cheering the girls and booing the boys. On the sidelines the boys who were old enough smoked Sweet Caps or rolled their own from little cotton bags of Bull Durham.

Do our Hatley diversions sound excessively mild? I'm afraid they must. Pleasures have changed in pace since then, and the radius of pleasure-seeking has stretched and stretched. But no plane which deposits you (and everybody else with you) on a distant coral strand can yield the delight we found in a green cove at the end of a three-mile paddle.

IX

I too will something make
  And joy in the making;
Altho' to-morrow it seem
Like the empty words of a dream
  Remembered on waking.

—ROBERT BRIDGES

HERE AND THERE THE PEAK OF SOME WORLD EVENT shows on my early horizons, but only because it links somehow into my own experience. The ending of the nineteenth century and the beginning of the twentieth caused vast public concern. Some looked forward to it with apprehension, as a natural date for God to put an end to a world which must have greatly disappointed Him; others expected it to usher in a new era of enlightenment and harmony. But when, exactly, was the transition to be? There was discussion among churchmen as to whether the right date to observe would be midnight of December 31, 1899, or of December 31, 1900—the latter being the end of the year that actually rounded out the nineteenth century from the birth of Christ. The dispute was settled by common consent when the new calendars for 1900 appeared; everybody forgot technicalities and prepared to enter the new millennium with either unusual solemnity or unusual gaiety. I knew nothing of the erudite discussions, of course, but was touched by the general excitement and disappointed not to be allowed to stay up for the watch-night service at Grace Church. I expected that some sort of miracle would occur and was indignant at having to miss it.

I was impressed during our first summer at North Hatley by how often we prayed for Queen Victoria. Her death the following winter therefore seemed to deserve special attention. The result was my first effort at news distribution, a bulletin circulated gratis to the family:

I see in my mind's eye, although the *Times* was even more chary then than it is now of using splurgy head-lines, the news of the terrible eruption of Mt. Pelée, in Martinique, as spread across the paper lying at my father's place when I came down to breakfast one morning in the spring of 1902. Over forty thousand people had been buried under a blanket of lava and ash. Four years later the memory of this catastrophe was fixed in my mind when I saw the streets of Naples piled with cinders and ashes after one of the worst eruptions of Mt. Vesuvius in modern times.

Boarding an ocean liner knowing I was actually going to sail down the harbor brought true the longings I had so often had when I hid my skates behind a crate on the dock and marched up the gangplank, posing as a bona fide passenger and trying to imagine what it would feel like to be one. Our ship was not a famous ocean grey-hound but the leisurely *Republic,* setting forth on one of the Mediterranean crossings that were the equivalent in those days of modern cruises. Captain Macaulay, with a grey beard, lively eyes and a capacious hug, gave me and a little girl named Caryl the freedom of the bridge, and when her bright red tam-o'-shanter blew overboard produced what seemed to me a most brilliant joke. "I'll pick it up," he said, "on the way back."

An actual taste of the delights of travel on a wider radius than Seabright in one direction and Quebec in the other gave me new ambitions. If at seven or eight I had had plans for a career like that of my friends the policemen or firemen I now at twelve dropped them; this visit to Italy with my mother and Margaret convinced me I must do something which would take me to far places. In Pompeii and Rome I decided that the most exciting life possible would be that of an archaeologist (and as I turn up a bit of Sassanian stucco with my toe or bend jungle undergrowth aside to glimpse a

Khmer sculpture the fever of discovery revives and for a moment I think I was right). Home again, however, I realized that I might have set my sights too high. Someday I would have to earn a living. How could I do this and still have a chance to see the world? Perhaps in the steamship or travel business. I began clipping every coupon that offered free leaflets about any sort of trip, if only to Saratoga or the Thousand Islands.

At boarding school that autumn none of these ambitions met with encouragement. The nearest thing to archaeology in our studies was an occasional line-cut in our Latin grammar ("Pompey Bust in the Forum" was a source of much merriment), and even geography was missing, since we were expected, wrongly, to have covered that earlier. But there was a school magazine, and my first appearance in print was an account of how we drove along the Bay of Naples to Torre del Greco, at the foot of Vesuvius. The lava had flowed up the aisle of the parish church but stopped at the foot of the altar; the populace were bringing paper flowers and saying prayers in thanks for the miracle. Further on, where the ground was still warm under foot, I purchased a five-centesimi piece that had been pressed into a black lump of molten lava. I was proud of my literary success in describing these adventures and saw that here also was a line of activity that might take me to far places.

I have always had a rather special feeling about Italy. It was inherited in a general way, of course, from my father, but I began at least half-consciously making it my own in the course of this first visit. Years later it became necessary to separate out what Mussolini meant by "Italy" from Italy past and Italy to come. In the

Fascist era, I sat one day before Mussolini in that great empty hall of his in the Palazzo Venezia. For an hour I listened to him sneer at everything I had been brought up to think of as having made his country glorious, and walked out shivering. But as I went down the marble stairway, furious at myself for being impressed even for the moment, I remembered one autumn evening at North Hatley when my father was sitting by the fire, deep in Trevelyan's story of Garibaldi and The Thousand. As he became more and more aroused he couldn't resist reading aloud from it even though this interrupted everyone else who was reading too. Could Mussolini's thugs be the successors of The Thousand? As soon as I was out in the sunshine of the Piazza Venezia I was again sure of the answer.

Actually, it was not in Italy but the Azores that the *Republic* landed us first. As the blue islands rose on the horizon I felt an excitement like that of an explorer at his first landfall, and I assumed everyone else on the ship shared it. Exactly fifty years later, a lady who had been on the *Republic* wrote to tell me that though her eyes had failed and she no longer could read *Foreign Affairs* she was glad to think that I was "still busy providing people with needed information"; and she recalled how on that particular morning I had hunted her and her husband up in a sheltered corner on the "wrong" side of the ship, piping out reproachfully:

"*Haven't* you seen the Azores? They've been there for *half an hour!*"

When the tender put us ashore at Ponta Delgada there was a great stir on the waterfront, but less notice was taken of us as we walked up the little street edged with pale pink and blue houses overhung with rampant magenta bougainvillaea. The inhabitants considered a street a place to sit in, eat in, drink in, gossip in, not just to hurry along. To my regret, nobody even offered to sell us a postcard. The air was humid, the feathery foliage motionless, and the loquats and other tropical fruits in the little garden where we sat in the shade not like anything I had ever known. I had been right to imagine myself an explorer; it was a new world to see and even more to feel.

A menacing pall of smoke was still hanging over Vesuvius as we came into the Bay of Naples, and ashore the streets were piled with powdery ash as snow used to be piled for weeks in New York; carts drawn by placid white oxen were very slowly carrying it off.

In Naples I noticed a work of art for the first time and realized that to look at something beautiful is a pleasure. I can pinpoint this moment of recognition as exactly as Harold Nicolson does the stirrings within him which later on he realized had marked the kindling of the tiny spark that informed him life was short and art was long. His discovery came one evening as he was walking with his aunt down a dark London street and suddenly saw before him a shopwindow full of glowing picture frames. The source of my discovery was the "Listening Dionysius" in the Naples Museum. I bought a photograph of it, took it home and thumbtacked it up in my hall bedroom in Tenth Street. Whenever I have been in Naples since then I have made a point of stopping in to see Dionysius, and although the names given him have varied he still seems to me one of the most graceful things ever made by human hands. At the same time I was also struck by Breughel's "Blind Leading the Blind," but this may have been mainly because of its drama.

The miracle of the lava, which as my own eyes had seen stopped short of the altar, was one thing; but the miracle which I was assured took place in the Church of Santa Chiara was another. Twice a year the dried blood of the martyred St. Janarius, preserved on the high altar in a silver reliquary, is believed to liquefy, and the faithful and even the unfaithful make it the occasion for a great popular festival. Images of the Madonna and companion saints are brought from all over Italy and carried around the aisles, while a great throng waits anxiously both inside the church and outside, for if the miracle is announced to have occurred speedily it is a good portent for the harvest and for other business affairs, while if there is a delay the outlook is bad. By going to the church early we were able to sit on the very steps of the altar, and once there were immobilized for the duration. The crowd gossiped good-humoredly, ate their bread and cheese and cracked their hard-boiled eggs on the marble pavement. As hour after hour passed they became impatient, and their supplications to the saint not to delay giving them a good omen began to be mixed with imprecations and threats. At last a priest suddenly rang a bell to signify that the blood had liquefied. The stalled procession began moving again, the crowd pressed forward to touch the figure of some especially admired saint, as joyous as a minute before they had been furious.

The voyage home on the *Moltke,* which we boarded at Genoa, was not as satisfactory as the voyage out. We were at sea on the Fourth of July, and I was outraged that the German band ignored my plea for "The Star-Spangled banner."

"If you *have* to," I said, "play the German anthem too, to keep things even."

When even this suggestion was not accepted, the impression about the manners of Germans which I had formed when we stopped for a night on the way from Naples to Paestum was not improved. We had put up at a small hotel at Cava dei Tirreni and were having dinner under a rose arbor when a large German family led by the grandmother trooped in and seated themselves along the opposite side of the table. The old lady managed the macaroni without difficulty, but when the meat and vegetables arrived she took from her reticule a steel machine in the shape of a large double fork that worked like a nutcracker; into this she fed everything on her plate, premasticated it there, piled it all into a grey mound and then ingested it as I imagined a python might, without chewing. It wasn't long before we left the table. Another count against the *Moltke* was that access to the bridge was strictly forbidden, which meant that there was little chance of spotting that red tam-o'-shanter.

My recollections of my two boarding schools are mixed. I had been headed for St. Mark's, like Maitland and Noel, but meantime it had become too expensive. The school I first went to in Connecticut was new and might have done well, but it changed hands. The second school in Maryland was larger and better. Since my day it has provided football stars for Princeton and other colleges, but the school teams in my time were nothing exceptional, as indicated by the fact that I played left tackle although I can't have weighed much more than a hundred and ten pounds. I liked soccer better, though it added new scars to those my shins already bore from roller-skating tumbles.

Not long after my first arrival at school I mentioned in a letter home that on warm Saturday mornings some of the boys rode over on their bikes to swim in a neighboring lake. I alluded to this with elaborate casualness, for bicycles were expensive. When my letter came, my mother, not giving the matter much thought, had Marion's old bicycle brought up from the cellar—the only one still there—and sent it along to me by express. I watched with horror as the station agent wheeled it out from the baggage room. However, I resisted the impulse to slide it off a small bridge nearby and instead pushed it the long way back to school—for I didn't know how to ride—steeling myself as I went along for the ordeal I foresaw ahead. A chivalrous senior who guessed my suffering said loudly that a girl's bicycle was as good as any other; and he taught me to ride, running behind with his hand on the saddle till I could keep my balance. In time the joke wore off, and I dare say I enjoyed the swims all the more because of their cost.

One small happening at school shows the change in social habits from that day to this. Fifty years ago divorce was not accepted as a possible solution for family disagreements, and as a boy I hardly knew it existed. A generation earlier the wife of one of my uncles had gone off with another man who happened also to be his best friend; but after the divorce that followed the uncle had lapsed into obscurity and subsequently died, so that by my time there was no occasion to refer to the affair; and indeed it was not referred to, so that I learnt of it only later from family papers. Now divorce came into my ken as an actuality. We heard with lively interest that the mother of one of my classmates, who happened to be a well-known portrait painter, was coming to visit him. We were told she was divorced, and none of us had ever seen a divorced person. I don't know what distinctive characteristics we expected would set her off from other women. At any rate, when she invited two or three of us to supper at the village inn we found that she was unusually elegant, beautiful and kind, which put the whole matter of divorce in a new light.

The worst time of my life, harder to get through than anything later, was when I broke the school honor system. I was in the Latin teacher's study, making up lessons missed through sickness while he worked on a paper for our next examination. When he went out of the room I was drawn almost automatically, at any rate irresistibly, to look at it. This was unnecessary; Latin wasn't one of my hard subjects. I must have seemed flustered when he came back; at any rate he asked me:

"D-d-did you l-l-look at the p-p-paper on my desk?"

He stammered, and now worse than usual.

It was a wrench, but I managed to say, "Yes."

"Do you r-r-realize I m-m-must t-t-t-tell the head-master?"

He was a nice man, and he could hardly get it out.

"Yes," I said again.

The headmaster gave me a choice. I could leave the next day; he would write the facts to my father; nobody else would know. Or he would announce in assembly that I had broken the honor system, and that between leaving the school quietly or having this public announcement made in my presence I had chosen the latter. I thought of my father and said I would stay. That night I didn't sleep, I knew my life was ruined, and in the morning I sat numb in assembly, gripping the sides of my desk, wondering how I could live through the next few minutes and, worse, how I could ever live afterwards. Only one boy turned around to look at me, and his neighbor kicked him hard. All were put on their honor not to tell the tale out of school. None spoke to me about it, though some gave me a friendly poke, and I suppose in time it was forgotten, except by me.

This was the blackest moment of my life, but as I look back I see that other shadows too, though of a different sort, lay across a path that on the whole was sunny and led through a landscape that seemed tidy and secure. Margaret once said, "As a family we are much given to conjecture." Conjecture too much indulged in easily becomes apprehensiveness. Perhaps one reason it did so in my case was that my mother and father were so much older than the parents of my friends. I did not figure, of course, what this might mean in terms of years, but as I grew up I nevertheless came to realize that things as they were would last considerably less than forever.

The realization sometimes came over me with a smothering rush. In the first summers at North Hatley, Papa now and then would take me alone for early supper on some small beach up the lake. It was then that I really heard what Danskammer had been like when he was my age. Once, when we had started a fire just big enough to boil a teakettle, and he was lying back, looking up through the birches, talking of the fun he had had with his brothers, their games, the traps they set, their skating on the River and shooting in the woods, recalling the names of their horses and their dogs, suddenly, with a shock of understanding, I realized that those brothers and every other living thing he spoke about were dead and gone, and that he was the last, the last. As I looked at his brown hand, with its splotches of freckle and its firm slender fingers, on one of them the familiar seal ring, I felt I could never make up to him "for everything" in the short time that I supposed he still had to live—shorter in my imagination than was actually the case.

I may have had something of the same feeling toward my mother too. My brother Bayard's death when he was not yet three had been a blow from which she never really recovered. To spare her feelings his name was seldom mentioned. But the two-handled mug from his godfather, Mr. McKim, was there as a silent reminder, kept filled with flowers by my mother as long as she lived. In his brief time on earth Bayard had made such an impression on the family that fifty years later Helen could say to me quietly, "I miss him still." If anything could have increased my love for my mother it would have been an instinctive feeling that she hoped to find in me a second Bayard; and with it would have come the apprehension that however much I might try I never could fill that place. I tried too hard, not only at that but at other things.

It was at school and, as must often happen, by chance, that I began experimenting with serious writing. As an editor of our school magazine, I thought of getting contributions in the form of little essays from all sorts of well-known persons—President Hibben of Princeton and Dr. Lyttleton, the famous headmaster at Eton, Jules Jusserand, the French Ambasador in Washington, Bishop Brent of the Philippines, Sir Hiram Maxim, artist friends of my father's like Edwin H. Blashfield and Elihu Vedder, and so on. My cheekiness, combined with the natural willingness of nice men to oblige a boy and the temptation to give advice to a younger generation, brought me over a dozen contributions. After they had been published under the running head "Talks to Boys," I got permission of the authors to send some of them to *St. Nicholas*. Such is the confidence of youth, matching my cheekiness in asking for free contributions, that I was hardly surprised when the group of articles was accepted; but I was overwhelmed when I received a check for one hundred dollars. Should I split it fifty-fifty with the ten contributors? Consultation with one of the masters salved my conscience in keeping it all instead of sending five dollars to each of the eminent gentlemen concerned.

This happy experience was of course no evidence of any literary ability of my own, but emboldened by it I determined to send *St. Nicholas* a piece I had written about one of my youthful heroes, "Chinese" Gordon. I had been moved by seeing how in St. Paul's Cathedral in London there always were flowers about Gordon's monument—not the formal wreaths deposited by patriotic organizations nearby at the feet of Wellington, but little nosegays, sometimes of country flowers. My sister Helen, to whom I owed this trip to England (as well as two others that we made together in my summer vacations), told me about Gordon's character of extraordinary contradictions and how the news of his death in Khartoum at the hands of the Mahdi's fanatics had raised a storm of anger and remorse in England from Queen Victoria down. She gave me a book of Gordon's letters and the Boulger biography.

With no more basic information than this, but with zeal and devotion, I wrote a short article about a man who must have been a hero to many other boys before and since. One piece of luck I did have. I got encouragement and some useful sidelights from a family friend, Colonel Prout, who had served in the Sudan as Governor of Equatoria Province and had known Gordon. As I look back, the fifty-dollar check I received from *St. Nicholas,* the first reward for writing of my own, still looms as the biggest I ever got in my life. One of the boys in school couldn't understand how it happened.

"You got fifty hard dollars," he said, "for just making that up out of your head?"

Colonel Prout wrote me that he approved my story except on one point. I had given my imagination rein and spoken of the mysterious dawn of the East that was breaking as Gordon faced the wild Arabs who had been hacking to pieces every human being they could find in the city and now hesitated at the foot of the palace stairs before rushing up to spear him to death. The notion that there is anything different or mysterious about nature's performances East or West is, he said, bosh. Today I remain doubtful. Is it purely my imagination that night falls abruptly in the desert and that dawn there is strange compared to that in northern climes?

Later my father took me to the old Fifth Avenue Bank, then in a pleasant brick and brownstone building, and introduced me to his friend Mr. Frissell, who endorsed my first deposit and ordered the opening of my account. "Small accounts," he said optimistically, "have a way of growing."

Since it was impossible to be with Helen without acquiring new ideas and tastes my trips with her abroad were important. She knew what she wanted to see, and her choice was good; she also knew what she wanted to avoid (this included any structure on which Sir G. G. Scott had laid his restoring hand), and this saved disappointments. Her English and her French history were not simple records of events; facts, though accurate, were secondary to the character and relationships of persons who had become alive for her in endless memoirs and novels. (I never knew anyone else who was not confused by the Wars of the Roses.) She never told you facts schoolmasterishly or directed you to look at this or that detail; she looked, and you could look too. She took things in quickly; she might go back for a second look at something, but meanwhile didn't dawdle while you wandered into a room ahead.

Our first trip took us north from London to Edinburgh by way of Cambridge (my first sight of the Backs), the great cathedrals (Durham, on its height, for me the noblest of all) and the grassy ruins of Fountains Abbey. In St. Giles's Church I seem to have reacted rather prissily to the Saint-Gaudens memorial to Stevenson; I wrote Papa that it didn't seem suitable in a religious setting.

In travelling, Helen wore a neat shepherd's-plaid suit

with a tight skirt slit an inch or two on one side, just not showing the knee. This was ahead of the fashion in rural parts and sometimes attracted attention. Of this she was quite unconscious, but she was abashed when a tall and evidently extremely farsighted London bobby stopped traffic to come over and, keeping his eyes carefully elevated, murmur, "Madam, your placket is open." And indeed, some of the *presse-boutons* on her skirt had come undone. Having decorously accomplished this service he returned to his post and traffic resumed.

The following summer while we were in Derbyshire we took lodgings for a few days at Rowsley with Mrs. 'Oward, across from the Peacock Inn. Sunday morning we walked over the fields to Haddon Hall. During lunch at the inn three of the prettiest girls I had ever seen (or ever have seen) came in with a governess and sat at the next table. The old waiter said they lived at Haddon Hall. Forty years later I could tell Lady Diana truthfully that I had never forgotten her face. From Derbyshire we went south to Ludlow, then took a boat at Monmouth to half-row, half-float, down the River Wye. Afterwards we went in leisurely fashion by coach along the Devon and Cornwall coast—Porlock and Lynton, Clovelly and Tintagel. Today they may be too-favorite haunts of trippers, but we were ahead of the motor charabancs. On the long hills we jumped out to lighten the load. And at even the smallest inns there was clotted cream with strawberries.

Our first morning at Conway, in North Wales, as we were starting out for a walk, a ruddy-faced Anglican Bishop asked if he might join us. We had gone only a short distance when he inquired what school I went to.

"I'm afraid you wouldn't know the name," I said. "It isn't at all famous."

"I know *all* the English schools," he replied.

"But this isn't English," I said.

"Why not?" he asked in surprise.

"I'm American, so I go to school in America," I said.

The Bishop was silent for a few steps, then murmured under his breath, "Not the slightest tinge." And afterwards, "Strange." Shortly he declared that he was becoming rather fatigued and turned back, leaving us to go forward at our usual quicker pace. We saw him again only at a distance.

Part of another summer we spent in France. Our ambition was to drive through Brittany in a donkey cart. To start with, however, we went to Paris, and from the first I found it perfect. They say London is the man's town, made to love and live with for life. For me, it is Paris that wears well, in all seasons, weathers, lights. We were in a modest hotel off the Etoile. In the morning the street bubbled with clear water, backed up in the gutters by little burlap dams. At noon the shine of the Champs Elysées was splendid; shops had not invaded it yet and carriages outnumbered cars. In the afternoon as we strolled along toward Rumplemeyer's little boys in unbelievably short and tight trousers were shovelling in the sandboxes and long-legged little girls were decorously playing with battledores or rubber balls they had brought in string nets (afterwards I recognized them as all having been Gilberte). In the evening the gas lights silvered the under sides of the horse chestnuts, making dim canopied aisles up and down which trooped beautifully and flimsily dressed young ladies, giving as they passed what seemed most friendly and unpremeditated "allos." We saw *Chantecler,* which I thought faintly ridiculous, and *Cyrano,* with the son of the great Coquelin. It was a minor misfortune that I imprudently picked up a peach at breakfast at the Hôtel Lotti (itself an imprudent choice, far from our own inexpensive hotel) and had to pay five francs for the privilege of having squeezed it and found it too hard to be edible. In the Place de la Concorde we regretted to think that Strasbourg must forever remain draped in mourning. (It was about this time that Price Collier wrote a book pronouncing France degenerate, a country of women without virtue, men without honor; and almost at once came the Battle of the Marne.)

From Paris we went to Reims and Laon, where, though we did not know its portent, the tramp of troops in the moonlit street kept us awake all night, and thence to Coucy-le-Château. Here Helen tried once again to start me sketching; but I knew better than to persist even though she pushed veracity so far as to praise the pencil drawing I made of the great donjon tower, the largest I believe in all Christendom, which then still kept guard over the valley of the Oise. The Germans were soon to destroy it. When we reached Brittany, the donkey we thought we had engaged was not waiting for us at Dol, and we had to reconcile ourselves to non-Stevensonian forms of locomotion. At Pont-Aven we stayed at the inn where Papa had spent a summer painting many years before, and made long walks at Locmariaquer, with its grey dolmens on a grey moor.

In one of the Christmas holidays my father took me

to my first opera. It was *Rigoletto* at the new Manhattan Opera House, where Hammerstein had set out to show the Metropolitan how stodgy it was. The audience here was less staid and less glittering than at the rival Met, and already in the first act was shouting its delight at Bonci's "Questa o quella." But this was only warming up for "Donna è mobile," which brought such roars from every part of the house that the professional claque stationed just behind us seemed opening their mouths silently. In the tumult that drowned the last notes of Melba's "Caro nome" I might have gone over the brass rail of the peanut gallery if my father hadn't held on firmly. Even today I could find my way to those seats, close under the ceiling and far around to the left, where no handicap on sight or sound kept me from identifying myself with every moment of tragedy on the microscopic stage far below.

Sarah Bernhardt was more exciting in theory than fact. My father thought I "ought to have seen her," and took me to a performance on one of her supposedly final tours at which she did acts from *L'Aiglon* and *Phèdre*. He had often seen her in Paris, and what was more (he emphasized) had heard her—for her voice had always been one of her chief weapons of conquest. Now it was shrunk, the magic was gone, and he was sorry he had not left his old impressions intact. This was before Bernhardt had one of her legs amputated, and she therefore was not handicapped as she must have been afterwards playing the boyish Roi de Rome in skin-tight breeches. Nevertheless I was disappointed, too, but said to myself, well, fifty years from now I can say I saw the divine Sarah; as now I do.

My first plays were *Secret Service* and *Held by the Enemy,* and no later scene has ever excelled in melodrama the one in which William Gillette, his right hand blown away, continued serenely to tap out the crucial message in Morse code. All children were supposed to love *Peter Pan* but I did not. It wasn't because of the horrible Captain Hook; he was so grotesquely ferocious as not to be believable. It was because I could see the wire that carried Maude Adams aloft, and I felt not just defrauded but annoyed that you were expected to be taken in by that sort of thing.

In those days there was a good stock company at the old Murray Hill Theater, on Lexington Avenue, nearly opposite the house of our close family friends, the Shippens. On red-letter Saturdays when I was taken there for lunch we would go over afterwards to a matinee. Frances Starr, Dorothy Donnelly and other good players made their first reputations there. Sometimes "Dick" Davis, very much a celebrity, was at lunch, and once when he found that I took an interest in theatrical stars he sent me a packet of autographed photos of various friends—Ada Rehan, Lillian Russell, Carmencita, Anna Held, besides others now forgotten. Alas, my interest seems not to have been enough to preserve them. The last time I remember them they were strung up on a cord in my room at school, where I hoped they would indicate the sort of life I was familiar with in the holidays. The illusion was helped when, acting on a dare, I sent a letter to Mary Garden and got back not a little reproduction like the ones movie stars now send out by the thousands but an enormous sepia photograph inscribed to me as not merely a connoisseur of music but apparently as an intimate friend.

X

Life, life's too weighty?
Too long a haul, sir?
I lived past eighty.
I liked it all, sir.

—STEPHEN VINCENT BENÉT,
"Thomas Jefferson"

NEVER IN MY LIFE DID I HEAR ANYONE IN MY family speak of doing anything "to pass the time." When Helen was quite old and with more energy left than strength, I asked her her idea of Heaven.

"Perpetual activity," she said, "without fatigue."

It was an answer Papa would have echoed. He could never find time to squeeze in all the things he wanted to do, a fact which I think goes far toward explaining why he had such a satisfactory life. He brought up a large family through his own efforts, an unusual achievement for an artist in America at that time, or indeed at any time, especially for an artist endowed with taste and talent but not genius. When reverses came he did not lament but set himself to find ways to overcome them. Above all, he took pleasure in almost everything. But the chief pleasures were those that came to him through the eye.

Bernard Berenson, commenting on Goethe's visit to Italy toward the end of the eighteenth century, said that as a sightseer Goethe seemed to have been blind to the Middle Ages. He rode through Monreale without pausing to look at the Byzantine frescoes and in Assisi had no word for Giotto or Cimabue. Girgenti, yes—there he went into raptures, justified certainly, but how much was it because classical remains were admired in his epoch and in the cultural climate in which he belonged? Goethe's love of nature was passionate. But Berenson points out that in his enjoyment of it "only the fore-edge seemed to exist"; the further distance of mountains, the skyline, lay outside the landscape that he noticed. Berenson did not intend, of course, to disparage Goethe's genius or his aesthetic sensibilities, but to emphasize the influence which fashion and habit may have on even very great minds and to illustrate what a vast distance can separate cultural appreciations in different ages.

Though my father was far from being as erudite as Berenson he shared with him the charming characteristic of eclecticism. He was not trammelled in bestowing aesthetic loves or gaining aesthetic delights by preconceived ideas, cultural tradition or native environment. His eye for beauty was continuously fresh. Nor did he merely observe it with critical apreciation; he felt it, whether the beauty was of Girgenti or Monreale, of Bellini or Cézanne, of the line of the Alban hills or the blue mass of Mt. Orford. He had no need of Housman's advice that when you are drinking barolo in Turin you should not reflect that there is better wine in Dijon. Late in life he worked with joy among his crowded flower beds in Quebec without stopping to be nostalgic for the more tender Italian climate or the broader Danskammer gardens.

One day in the Jeu de Paume recently I realized what a pity it was that impressionism had not reached him in his formative years. But I noted that even so one of Gauguin's pictures there, a scene of haymakers in Brittany painted as late as 1888, makes no more use of atmosphere and rather less of light than did some of my father's painting at Pont-Aven or on Newport beach years earlier. He was attracted to work in glass, I think, by the opportunities it gave for luminosity and depth of color, and these are the qualities that mark the most successful of his windows, as also those of his friend La Farge. His mosaics also were as fine as any made till then in this country, as shown by the delicate and intricate design in sepia, cream and gold above the altar in the Church of the Ascension in New York. One of his best windows is nearby, next to one of La Farge's best; and it does not suffer by comparison.

I wouldn't pretend to say what might have been his opinion of some of the art produced today. I do recall, though, the stir created by the Armory Show and how "Nude Descending a Staircase" was the subject of discussion at lunch in Tenth Street—not ridicule but discussion, critical, analytical, but not dogmatic. That was the prevailing attitude there in questions of taste. A thing was not condemned because it was new any more than it was praised because it was new. Nor did its monetary value have anything whatever to do with whether it was considered beautiful. A bit of pottery with an apple-green glaze or an Etruscan vase that my father saw a peasant turn up while he was riding on the Campagna was not comparable to the Madonna from Donatello's studio that he bought in Florence, considered either in light of the thirty-five francs he paid for it then or the thousandfold of that value it might have now. But he looked at each for what it was and saw in it its individual quality and worth.

A chance for him to use this ability to look at things with an unconformist eye came when he was appointed Director of American Fine Arts at the Paris Exposition of 1878. He and Saint-Gaudens, who was his assistant there, determined to give Europeans a first view of the generation of American painters who were breaking with the traditions of the Hudson River School. They had been authorized to select works in Paris to supplement those chosen by an academic jury in New York, and they seized on this to add pictures by Mary Cassatt, Winslow Homer, La Farge, Elihu Vedder and George Inness. What was more, they hung these pictures of relatively unknowns on the line and "skied" established favorites. This surprised Paris, which till then knew nothing of such American work. There was as much applause in Europe (the French government gave my father the Legion of Honor) as there was condemnation in conventional art circles at home.

Saint-Gaudens was then living in Paris, working on his Farragut. Earlier that year he had finished a small bas-relief of my father, the first of the many he afterwards made, and one of the best. He sent it to him in New York as a surprise present with an accompanying letter.

"This is a portrait," he wrote, "of one of my best friends; rather a short man, a heavy mustache, an open eye—Mr. La Farge said that his face looked in parts as if it were 'tied up in a knot'—notwithstanding that he's a pretty good kind of fellow. The gentleman I mean is not two steps from where you stand, and I give it to him as a slight token of esteem and affection."

Though my father lived an artist's life while studying in Paris with Luc Olivier Merson (he was Merson's first pupil) and painting with friends in Pont-Aven it never occurred to him to transplant the velvet jackets and berets that came naturally in those surroundings to his New York studio or glass shop. He thought that artists who affected long hair and sloppy clothes were compensating for lack of serious talent by appearing bohemian. Mannerisms take time, the pretense of not paying attention to conventions as much as any other, and he was too busy for them.

I was not allowed to bother him while he was working in his studio on Washington Square, but that was made up for when now and then I went to the glass shop. It was an enormously high room, with bins of glass lining one side and sheets of glass propped up everywhere. The glass had been made according to his directions, and it was of every variety of hue and texture imaginable. On one side was the oven where the painted glass was fired, a delicate operation. Shafts of light slanted down from the glowing parts of an unfinished window. Papa would be up there, directing things from the top of a ladder. The head workman, Mr. Hart, would hold up one piece of glass after another from a certain bin. Papa would reject and reject until at last, satisfaction showing in his china-blue eyes, he found precisely what he had in mind. The cutter would then shape it to fit the design on the full-size cartoon, brushing the remnants onto the floor in a tinkling shower. The whole would be fixed together eventually with snaky lengths of lead, secured at the joints with solder. I left with a glass jewel or a bit of ruby glass cut for me into a heart or diamond.

At the glass shop Papa worked briskly, and the workmen did also by the contagion of his enthusiasm. It was his habit all his life to move rapidly. At seventy he was still running up and down stairs just as he had done always. And the one extravagance he continued to allow himself to almost the end of his life was to keep his horse "Warrenton" at Durland's and ride him regularly in Central Park.

Thus it was an energetic atmosphere in which the children were brought up, the older ones particularly. Not much distinction was made between boys and girls as to what was expected of them or what they were allowed to do. This did not mean that the girls were tomboyish; Margaret and Helen were as much the reverse of that as Maitland and Noel were the reverse of being sissy. If I was in danger of being the latter the older ones were there to see that it shouldn't happen. As a family friend, Eloise Bergland, explained to me: "You grew up with the equivalent of two uncritical grandparents and five aunts and uncles determined not to let them spoil you."

Margaret and Helen were remarkable women. As Margaret was the elder she got her start as an artist first —to be exact at sixteen, when she began painting dinner cards, menus and such and sending them to New York to be sold at the Women's Exchange. Helen saw no reason not to follow and was soon doing the same. When they saw a Christmas card which Elihu Vedder drew and sent to my father they began the next year to draw and color Christmas cards too—innocent first drops of the present commercialized deluge. Their only education at Danskammer was from a cultivated English governess who taught them what she herself cared about—literature and English and French history; the mathematics was rudimentary and there was no science. They had no formal art lessons apart from the year of study that Helen had later on with William M. Chase in New York. At the start they were much influenced by Walter Crane and Kate Greenaway, but gradually developed along lines of their own. Margaret was the better at design, Helen at figures. Soon they were working professionally for New York publishers.

Thomas Wentworth Higginson, who edited Emily Dickinson's poetry and worked indefatigably for the emancipation of American women, wrote that "men have been willing to see any amount of literary or artistic genius developed in women—when these ladies have consented to attribute their work to a husband or brother, and say nothing about it." One thinks at once of exceptions; yet in fact the handicap of femininity was still strong in Victorian America when Margaret and Helen were beginning their careers. Nobody asked them to work anonymously or in someone else's name, and all they had to do to overcome the handicap of sex was to resort to a gentle subterfuge. They simply omitted to say that they were girls, and very young ones at that, and signed their work and their correspondence with their surnames and initials only. When letters came from publishers addressed "Mr." instead of "Miss" they did as Colonel Higginson would doubtless have advised and said nothing about it.

More or less by chance, Margaret found herself doing book covers. In those days nobody thought of dust jackets except as a means of keeping off the dust; as soon as you bought a book you took the paper jacket off. She started a vogue for making the book covers themselves artistic and distinctive, and her covers became a sort of identity tag for an author. Whenever I see the dark blue and gold design on the spine of some book on a library shelf I have recognized it as Henry van Dyck's even before Margaret's distinctive lettering tells me so. The remarkable thing is that almost all the hundreds and hundreds that she designed are original in conception and excellent in taste. In most cases she could follow her own wishes, but occasionally was called upon to match her style to that of the author, which might be terrible. Thus the saccharin mauve cover which she devised for the first Myrtle Reed novel was so exactly right that she had to perpetuate it with variations through all the rest of that immensely popular and long-forgotten author's string of works.

When she was already rather tired of this success she undertook something new that turned out to be quite an adventure. On a trip to the West she discovered that there was no field book of Western wildflowers, and she persuaded Major Putnam that his firm's well-known series of nature books should include one. Her plan was to do the illustrations for a handbook to be prepared by some well-known professor of botany. For this she was excellently equipped, since she was a good amateur botanist and drew with absolute accuracy as well as taste. But the professor commissioned for the task fell out and in the end could do no more than help with advice from his study. Could Margaret do the text as well as the illustrations? Nothing ever stumped her. She could. For three years she and two or three friends roamed all over the West, camping, walking and driving in the deserts of Utah and New Mexico, along the salty margins of the Pacific, on the edges of mountain snow, beside the waterfalls of the Yosemite and around the foot of Mount Rainier. "Ladies don't do that," said the park custodian when they planned to take their tents, sleeping bags and cooking equipment to spend several weeks on the plateau halfway down the Grand Canyon; but these ladies did. Elsie Littell has told me how Margaret would appear on a ledge with a flower in her mouth, and carefully make her way down using both hands, tuft by tuft, rock by rock; then, not waiting to brush the dust and burrs off her clothes, begin drawing the flower, perhaps one never correctly recorded, and making notes of the coloring. She drew all the flowers from life, and large numbers of them were described accurately for the first time. Today, after nearly fifty years, her book remains the standard work in its field.

But Margaret's most satisfactory achievement came twenty years later, when her versatile talent and endless energy turned into still another direction. Fanny Kemble's journals of life on a slave plantation in Georgia had always moved her; Fanny's adventurous nature responded sympathetically to hers. Now she began research into Fanny's family, life and times, the result of which was a biography which was taken by the Book-of-the-Month Club, praised by the critics and became a best seller. It was published when Margaret was over seventy, an age, wrote Steve and Rosemary Benét in a profile, "when most successful writers are quite ready to retire to the spiked couch of their collected editions." Margaret was never ready to retire. She followed Fanny's life with a life of one of Fanny's admirers, Trelawny, the friend of Shelley's, a man of extraordinary adventures. This too was taken by the Book-of-the-Month Club and became a best seller. Margaret and Helen had been living alone in Tenth Street since my parents' death. They thanked Fanny for giving the house three badly needed roofs and two new furnaces. But the financial success was nothing compared to Margaret's gratification in finding that she had not been insanely optimistic to launch out on a new career in her old age. The thought that it is possible to start fresh again at seventy should cheer anyone speeding along toward that milestone and cause him to look around for fresh pastures.

Helen's professional life, like Margaret's, covered more than fifty years. She wrote:

"I remember winter days at Danskammer when Papa would have a big sketch for a window to finish, with lots of tracery and ornaments to be outlined and colored. Margaret and I were about twenty then, and we would work with him at the big studio table. Everything was snug and warm, and as it grew late we would work faster and faster, for the coachman was waiting out in the snow with a horse saddled to catch the night mail at Marlborough. Lamps would be lighted and tea and cakes brought up, and then at last it was finished. There's no pleasure like finishing something, except working at it. I've worked under pressure most of my life, and liked it."

Gradually Helen became my father's principal helper and then his partner. She preferred painted to opalescent glass, and after he died turned mainly to that. Her opinion that publicity was detestable made her success all the more remarkable. Once I trapped her into a boast. "I never asked for work," she said. "It always came to me, more than I could do."

Painted glass is a gamble. A face on which Helen had worked for days might very well be cracked in the firing, and often was. This meant simply beginning over again. In the glass shop it was wonderful to see how she bent Mr. Hart and the other old German workmen to her very exacting will, giving her directions from the top of the long ladder where my father had been used to perch. She was tiny, not over five feet, slim and delicate. They adored her.

Helen's pleasures came more exclusively through the eye than did my father's. She read everything, new and old, and the old over and over; like Margaret, too, she liked people and conversation. But what gave her the most continuous pleasure was the look of things. She wasn't forever saying: "See the beautiful line of that hill," or "See the beautiful juxtaposition of those planes." She simply was seeing it and continuously getting pleasure from it. She would have joined Harold Nicolson in saying: "I am not dependent for my happiness on sound; only on sight." When Nicolson added that he couldn't tell Puccini from Beethoven she went him one better. Music did not exist for her; she found it a succession of meaningless noises, unpleasantly interrupting painting, reading and conversation.

My recollection of the Tenth Street studio is of concentrated activity. Margaret would be at work on a book cover at the big table in the center. What attracted me most among her painting equipment was the mussel shells in which gold was for some reason then sold, and may still be. Helen would perhaps be painting a panel of glass against the north window, or she might be on a stepladder working with long stalks of charcoal on a cartoon, crumbs scattering in all directions as she rubbed out a line with a chunk of fresh bread. I might have been called up there when I came home from school to put my foot on a big Webster's dictionary to help with a sketch of Christ on the steps of the temple, or a piece of stuff would be draped on my shoulder as it might have hung on one of the Wise Men from the East.

"Look up," Helen would say briskly. "Those chimneys out there on the Cowards' house are porphyry columns. You are advancing up a broad flight of steps to where the High Priest stands between them. Now don't teeter!"

Maud, the lay figure, was supposed to serve these purposes, but in her old age she usually sprawled in the corner under the deflated punching bag, her joints too weak to hold her in correct positions and her cotton stuffing protruding at the wrong places. She had to be salvaged, however, when I went to boarding school; and even before that my legs were too scarred and muscular from roller skating to be attractive models for anything.

When Helen stopped working at about seventy it was not because of lack of orders, energy or talent but following a dismaying experience. She was used to the eccentricities of clients, had dealt amicably with ladies as arbitrary as Mrs. O. H. P. Belmont (for whom she made a magnificent series of windows) and clergymen with strange ideas of what it was possible or suitable to depict in a window. (As my father said, "The clergy often appear to think they receive a special knowledge of art together with the other gifts of ordination.") This time the trouble was more serious. She received a commission from an enormously rich lady to do a series of windows for a private chapel being built on her place in the country. Helen borrowed fifty thousand dollars from a bank to finance the operation, which took about two years. The lady said she loved the windows, the architect pronounced them perfect, a cardinal came and consecrated the chapel, pictures were in all the papers; but months went by, a year went by, Helen was paying interest at the bank, and still the very rich lady neglected to send her check. Helen went through such a bad time imagining what would happen if it never came that she decided then and there not to undertake any more important commissions.

The business side of her work was a worry to Helen in any case, and it was always a problem what to do with the money she made beyond what was needed for current expenses. She was not in the advantageous situation of Mrs. Hoppin, J. P. Morgan's unworldly sister-in-law. When Mrs. Hoppin inherited a small sum of money she astounded Helen by coming to her and asking how she thought she ought to invest it.

"I'm the worst possible person to give advice on something of that sort," Helen said. "Why not ask Mr. Morgan?"

"Well, I suppose I *might,*" said Mrs. Hoppin, turning this original thought over in her mind dubiously. "He *is* bright and clever in those things."

Helen's own idea of stocks and bonds was that it was most misleading to call them "securities"; the right name was "risks."

Margaret and Helen were much the same size; each weighed about a hundred pounds, Helen a little less, Margaret a little more. They had trim figures and, within their means, dressed well. Fanny Kemble not only procured new furnaces for them in Tenth Street but new fur coats also. I never go down lower Fifth Avenue on a late winter's afternoon that I don't wish I saw that diminutive pair walking briskly along, with the loft buildings in the side streets to the west framing a flamboyant sky that particularly pleased Helen because it seemed so alien in those dingy canyons.

Their influence on me as I was growing up went far beyond encouraging a recognition of beauty in its many forms, a faculty that a child cannot be taught but in favorable circumstances can develop; the circumstances in my case were favorable in the extreme, and though I possessed no native artistic faculty that could be developed creatively, it was quickened enough to give me pleasure all my life. Far beyond this in importance was the influence of the simple presence of two such beings at the center of the scheme of things that I knew was the right one.

One of their friends, Sophie Kerr, made the flat statement in a letter to me: "Helen and Margaret were the most interesting women I ever knew." And Hugh MacLennan, a friend from Hatley days, wrote of Helen: "Every trace of sentimentality was alien to her." Besides having feeling without sentimentality, they had intellect without pride. They also had courage. The day Helen died she told me of a dream she had had the night before. She was fighting on Okinawa, fighting hard and winning—"and it was such a pleasure to be strong and to be winning." She had wanted to stop living, she said, when Margaret died. But then she could hear Margaret saying "Nonsense!" and had decided to live if she could, "even if it meant trying to eat more."

As children at Danskammer, Marion and Noel were as close as Margaret and Helen were later: Mary McGuire said she had never known two children of opposite "sects" who got along so well together. It was a loss for me that I saw Noel only intermittently. He was the most single-minded person I ever knew. It never occurred to him that what anyone might think of him was important, for it never occurred to him that anyone could help him or harm him. He took over the Danskammer farm, ploughed up a brickyard that had encroached on it, and came to New York as seldom as possible, content with his farm, his woods, his family, his gun. He tended the light on Danskammer Point in all weathers; it was part of the place where he belonged. Once when an old friend was talking with him the subject of death for some reason came in.

"Where would you like to die?" the friend asked.

"On Beacon Hill," Noel said.

The friend protested: "But all the little animals would gnaw your bones."

"Oh I'd like that," Noel said.

To say simply that my mother might have preferred a more conventional family would make her appear stuffy, and this would give a wrong picture, for though in many respects my family may sound conventional in the very different focus in which we view social forms today, it seemed far from that to contemporaries at the tag end of the Victorian era. In those days a family in which the husband and two daughters were professional artists did not conform to any proper norm. Nevertheless, I don't think it ever occurred to my mother to let that sort of thing trouble her; she was quite settled in her mind as to what was what and who was who in her New York. But she may very well have thought that it would be agreeable if the members of her family were a little more relaxed, and especially if they were less occupied with affairs of art in which she had no direct share. After producing seven children and bringing up six of them (my brother, Bayard, born between Noel and me, died in infancy), many ladies of her day would have spent much of their time on a chaise longue. Indeed, I remember that one of my aunts did exactly that, dressed in white silk with ruffles, a high white ruching around her neck and a crepe lisle cap with streamers. But Mamma was neither indolent nor an invalid, simply what now sounds terribly old-fashioned.

Fortunately, she needed to know little about the details of housekeeping. That lack was unimportant, because even when my father was very hard up, after the return from Rome and again later when he gave his accumulated capital to help Maitland out of a business failure (my father was not either legally or morally involved, but thought it right to do so), there were nice country girls near Danskammer ready to do all the household chores, and for Tenth Street there were plenty of Irish girls arriving by every boat and looking for a place to start; they had to be shown how to light the gas and use a coal stove, but they were good-natured and willing to learn.

The most surprising notation in Marion's diary at Danskammer was the entry: "Mamma has been painting the nursery." She did delicate things with her hands very well—embroidery and cross-stitch, mending books, and so on—but I never saw her attempt to hang a picture or use a paint brush, perhaps because usually someone else in the family thought he or she could do it better. The reader may here be tempted to say, "Poor Mamma." That would be unnecessary. She liked her family individually and collectively, simply might have been still more satisfied had they been less energetic in so many directions.

About cooking she knew nothing, though occasionally, I remember, she made some special dessert at Danskammer. This entailed considerable preparations. Everything would be brought into the dining room, where the table was covered first with paper and on top of that a linen sheet. Then Mamma would set about making "velvet cream," the liquid part of Damson preserves topped with whipped cream, poured into the tall old-fashioned champagne glasses from Venice, lovely spirals with thin lightblue edges. Or she might make "syllabub"—cream, wine, sugar and spice, beaten up with a fork and the bubbles skimmed off until a glass bowl was filled with nothing but bubbles.

She liked the country, but not as enthusiastically as my father did, for her outdoor activities were limited, particularly as she thought of horses only as providing a necessary but harrowing method of transportation. She took the children into the garden when they were small, or sat reading in the grape arbor, or picked rosebugs off her favorite Father Hugo rose, or in season gathered raspberries—"They're the right height."

Mamma was wonderful with little children but less good at managing older ones. This applied particularly to Marion, who grew up passionately liking everything she liked and passionately disliking everything she disliked. She disliked everything formal and in particular New York parties where she thought she wouldn't know people. Echoes would come down from the top floor as she argued frantically to get out of going to some dinner or ball by complaining that her old dress was a fright or that Margaret had done her hair horribly. Then when I came down early the next morning I would find the hall table heaped with loot she had left there for me, the favors from last night's cotillion; but she would never admit that she had had a good time. She was the only member of the family who was too intense to enjoy things. Her strong feelings upset Mamma, who remained very much the product of her mother's big brownstone house on Stuyvesant Square where in spite of the inevitable tragedies of sickness and death the pattern was stable and things were viewed in proportion. She quietly made the best of the things she didn't much like and quietly enjoyed the many more things she did like.

Helen said Marion had the nature of a genius, but with no focus and no outlet. "She ought to have been born without morals," she added. In spite of herself, Marion never lacked for beaux. She was determined not to let them imagine that she would take the slightest trouble to please them. Even in the city, when one came to call she would put on a rough skating dress and heavy boots and half-turn her back to make sure he wouldn't think she was glad to see him. Yet in spite of everything she was very attractive to men, not so much because she was so different as because as soon as she forgot to be rude she became vivid and amusing. The man who successfully persisted, Alfred Edey, made her happy, but all too soon died.

Marion's memory was prodigious, better even than Helen's. No conscious mental effort was involved; it seemed not to be the mind that remembered but the senses working in spontaneous accord. For her there was no threshold between childhood and maturity; life was a continuum in which all experiences stood out sharply, no one of them older or more blurred than another. In *Early in the Morning,* a book written when she was over seventy, she spoke of playing with the rector's children in the cellar of the Church of the Ascension, on the corner of Tenth Street and Fifth Avenue. Happening to peer out through a small grate on the level of the sidewalk, hardly more than a slit, she saw Mamma walking along on the other side of the street. She called out to her in excitement, but it was some time before Mamma could locate the muffled voice.

"Is it that tiny opening I pass every day," I asked her, "the one with square gratings?"

"Not at all," she said, holding up her two hands with fingers crossed to make diamonds. "The openings were lozenge-shaped."

The next morning I saw it was so. After sixty years she still felt her nose pressed against the iron grating, still saw the world outside divided into diamonds, definitely *not* squares.

By contrast with the days the evenings in Tenth Street were quiet, except for an occasional dinner party or unless old Maynard or old Nadal or old Howells (everyone seemed to me then as old as the hills) or some other friend of my father's came in. In the differently organized city of those times, it was the habit for members of the Century Club to spend Saturday evenings there, with congenial talk and a Welsh rabbit and a drink towards midnight. When Papa was about eighty I asked him why he didn't go there as regularly as in the past.

"Too many old codgers," he said.

On ordinary evenings when I came down to say good night after finishing my lessons I would find everyone reading. Papa would be in a comfortable armchair near a good lamp with something like Baring-Gould's *Tragedy of the Caesars* or *The Education of Henry Adams* (where can that early copy have disappeared to?) or perhaps a Peter Dooley or the latest Howells. Mamma would be on the sofa near the fire with something like *The Virginian* or *David Harum* or rereading Marion Crawford or a Henry James about Italy; she too never ceased loving Italy. Margaret and Helen would be reading anything, which meant everything; there were much fewer new books in those days and they seemed to read practically all of them, besides the old stand-bys. Helen liked to sit on "little red velvety," so-called even after its original covering had changed more than once. It was made from the last surviving pear tree in the orchard of what had been Governor Peter Stuyvesant's Bouwerie Farm. For over two hundred years the old tree stood at what in time became Third Avenue and Thirteenth Street. When at last it was overwhelmed by the distempers of city life, the governor's descendent, Uncle Petrus, made a small chair from the wood for each of his grandnieces, of whom my mother was one. When I sat down in the parlor, which was rare except on Sundays, I chose it if possible.

I have speculated sometimes as to why it was that my mother and father, despite their different tastes and temperaments, got along together so well. It was not because in those days married people, except in cases of extreme incompatibility, were expected to get along and hence as a matter of course saw to it that they *did* get along. It was not because both of them were well-bred and considerate, or even because they simply became used to each other. It must have been, I decided, because they loved each other all their married lives, up to and beyond a golden wedding, without reservation and without exception.

❧ XI ❧

O voyage fast!
O vanished past!
—GEORGE ELIOT,
"Two Lovers"

❧   REMEMBRANCE IS INTANGIBLE PROPERTY, WHAT
Vladimir Nabokov has called "unreal estate"—the most
valuable, as one grows older, of all one's belongings.
The manner in which our country lived a generation
ago, and the way in which our parents thought, are
gone as utterly as Nabokov's have gone. They did not
disappear all at once, as his did, in violent revolution.
The changes came gradually, each of them, it seemed,
for the good; but whether for good or ill, irresistibly
and with astounding cumulative effect.

In the years when I was growing up the new machines
and the new ways of life imposed by them were flooding
across the American landscape. Like the incoming tide
at Mont-Saint-Michel, which sends inch-high crests of
foam in slow succession across a vast expanse of flats
until suddenly when you look again what seemed like
terra firma is entirely lost to view, so the years since I

was a child have submerged the American scene that I remember. It is gone as finally as, when I myself was a child, the idea of my father's driving in *his* childhood in the family coach from Danskammer to Charleston was gone, indeed had become incredible and rather ridiculous. Without venturing a judgment that many of the things about the scenes of my own childhood were not ridiculous, even if today they are almost incredible, I have set down this rough inventory of them, my "unreal estate."